Pizza with Jesus
(No Black Olives)
Finding Hope and Grace
Amid Hardship and Grief

D1225594

Pizza with Jesus

(No Black Olives)
Finding Hope and Grace Amid Hardship and Grief

P.J Frick

Pizza with Jesus
(No Black Olives)
Finding Hope and Grace Amid Hardship and Grief

© P.J Frick 2017

Published by
P.J. Frick
Ingram Spark/Lightning Source LLC

Dedication

For my sweet, gentle David – a true man of God and a light of His love in this world.

Acknowledgments

Let the peace of Christ rule in your hearts, since as members of one body you were called to peace. And be thankful. Let the message of Christ dwell among you richly as you teach and admonish one another with all wisdom through psalms, hymns, and songs from the Spirit, singing to God with gratitude in your hearts. And whatever you do, in word or deed, do everything in the name of the Lord Jesus, giving thanks to God the Father through him.
– Colossians 3:15-17 (NIV)

A friend loves at all times…
- Proverbs 17:17 (NIV)

As an elementary school librarian, I start each class by asking students to give me "eyeballs and smiles"- my call sign that I am ready to begin the lesson. I scan each face and smile right back. By the time I get to the last face, I am smiling in and from my heart. I can feel myself just beaming back at them. It is overwhelming in the best way to see those smiling faces. Precious creations…My little people! I follow that up with an opportunity for students to share the good things happening in their lives – the moments and things that make them smile and/or stop for a moment of gratitude. So, it seems somehow fitting that I start this conversation with some of my good things. Many blessings and good things have surrounded me, held me up and led me to this place. Despite a seemingly endless onslaught of loss and hardship, it has not been all bad. I have smiled and laughed a lot along the way. Many people and moments have planted seeds of gratitude in my heart. Indeed, I have much to be grateful for.

One of the greatest blessings and comforts in my life, of course, was my sweet, gentle David – the kindest and best of men. He had a giant heart of service and lived a life of love. As always, he is helping me and others – even from beyond. This is his story. This is our story.

David and Me

My loving family has stood by me at every twist, turn and tunnel. ***Patti, Heather, Jim, Jason, Christopher, Justin, Jackson***: You have surrounded me with love and patience and forgiveness through this, the hardest time in my life. May you be blessed and comforted as you have blessed and comforted me.

Ken and Marie: You have taken me in as your daughter-in-law and loved me as if I were your own. You are truly good and faithful servants of our Lord, and you created a wonderful and faithful man in your loving son, David. May you find some comfort in knowing how much better this world is because of you and our gentle David.

My equally loving church family at Waxhaw United Methodist Church is the sweetest, most supportive adoptive family I could know. *My dearest church family*: You held and carried David and me throughout David's battle. You continue to hold me up during the ups and downs of the grieving process. You truly are the best! I thank God for you every single day.

My work family and the students at Lewisville Elementary School (LES) in Richburg, SC did not know me very long. Yet they took me right in and prayed with me, helped me shelve books, and surrounded me with smiles, love and encouragement. They worked with my disruptive schedule without complaint. I felt like I belonged there, and the sweet children made me feel like I was theirs. *Beth G., Linda M., Bridgette, Kim M., Leslie S., Teresa and Wanda*: I truly would not have made it through this time without your kindness, prayers, patience, and friendship. Thank you for believing in me. I will miss you always.

My barn buddies offer me a place of solace, humor and new, true friendships. *Kim, Michelle, Taylor, Jonathan, Allison and Lyn*: You give me something to look forward to every day.

My van clan continues to support and love me through everything. *Lisa, Larry and Sue, Donna, Judy, Phyllis and Mike*: Your friendship means the world to me. Even though we no longer ride to work together, I could not ask for better companions along life's journey.

Last but definitely not least, *my fur kids – past, present and future - (Maggie, Kittie, Matrix, Lucy, Tillman, Pup, Jeff and Sidney and Blaze)*: Your comforting presence has surrounded me with unconditional love even on the most difficult days. Your humorous antics have brought me daily smiles and laughter. Your snuggles have kept me warm and at peace. You have welcomed me home every day – just as you will when you greet me at Heaven's door. What a comfort!

There are not enough pages to name and thank the countless others who were part of this journey. So many people shared their time, gifts, resources and love. They took me out, brought meals and let me hang out in their barns: Cousin Marie Frick for the simple wooden cross and soft prayer shawl that comforted David; Pastor John and Anita McGill; Christie, Carter, Chris, Amy and O'Neill Plyler; the Ezzell family (especially big, gentle Buddy and sweet Margaret, Paula and Ben); the Howie family (Amy, Jim, Judy and Lester); Shirley and Bob Schmidt for all the hugs and chicken pot pies; Susan and John Johnson for all the hugs, sweet smiles and tomato pies; Greg Hart for the umbrella and constant encouragement; Susan and David Johnson; Terri and Joel Barbee; Gezell and Calvin Fleming; Shay and Ashley; Bonnie Hiate; Sonny and Elaine McManus; Becky Morgan for sharing her hard-won wisdom from her cancer journey; Belinda Lamm; Al and Nancy; Christopher Tucci; Judy Cline; Kim Thomas and Maximus for offering me a new and lasting friendship just when I needed one; Laura Arthur; Union United Methodist

Church; the doctors and staff at Novant Cancer Specialists and other Novant facilities; Dr. Humphrey and the staff at Ballantyne Veterinary Clinic. Thank you for your support, fellowship and prayers throughout this entire journey. You held David and me close. You held me up and pulled me through. You offered encouragement and advice. I am stronger and better for having gone through this time of suffering with all of you. I know David appreciates all of you, too!

Heavenly Father and Christ Jesus, my Lord, I pray...

Thank you, Father, for the gift of loving friends and caring others. In even the darkest times they shine their love to guide us back to you, give us hope, peace, and safe harbor. Without them this world would be a dark and lonesome, loathsome prison. In your wisdom, you cross our paths with others at just the right time and place to make your presence known and to remind us that you are here with us. You have not forsaken us. You are our rock and our foundation – always. We cannot be shaken. I expect, accept and appreciate the generous gifts of the universe which come only from you. Thank you for your wondrous love, grace, and redemption. Help us to take those gifts and carry them out into the world, shining your light of grace and love to others - and back to you. May we comfort and bless others as you comfort and bless us.

In Jesus' name,
Amen

Table of Contents

Chapter 1
Bootsie, Me and God

*The King will reply, "Truly, I tell you, whatever you did
for one of the least of these brothers and sisters of mine,
you did for me."*
– Matthew 25:40 (NIV)

He says, "Be still, and know that I am God."
– Psalm 46:10 (NIV)

*What do you think? If a man owns a hundred sheep, and
one of them wanders away, will he not leave the ninety-
nine on the hills and go to look for the one that wandered
off? And if he finds it, I tell you the truth, he is happier
about that one sheep than about the ninety-nine that did
not wander off. In the same way your Father in heaven is
not willing that any of these little ones should be lost.*
– Matthew 12:14 (NIV)

 God sends his angels and love in many forms. One
of my favorites is the dog. Always I learn from dogs – my
own and every single stray. Technically, all of my dogs
are rescues. In fact, they rescue *me* - daily. I aspire to be
as good, worthy, and true as they are - for they display
courage, humor, grace, and forgiveness in even the
darkest, most challenging situations. It is no wonder then

that a dog is the one who presented me with my latest "ah-ha" moment in my relationship with God and Jesus. God knows that the quickest way to my heart is through a dog.

Bootsie is a cute, blonde Lhasa-Apso/Poodle mix who was pulled from a local dog hoarding situation. Apparently, the dogs in that horrible place never got outside. So, naturally, Bootsie was shy - and now terrified. He escaped from his foster home's fenced yard and ran away. When I first saw Bootsie, it was a starry, damp-cold October night, and I was letting my own dogs out for their last out of the evening. Lucy, my old, round, white-ish Great Pyrenees/Retriever mix charged the fence and commenced to barking out her usual raucous notification that we were being invaded.

I honed in on the direction Lucy was barking and saw a blonde apricot blur just on the other side of the fence. I don't know who was more surprised at my seeing Bootsie, but I tend to think I would win that honor. Immediately I recognized Bootsie from a text and neighborhood e-mail I had seen earlier that day. I gasped and exclaimed (to nobody in particular), "Oh! Oh no! It's him! Oh! Wait!" In my haste, I almost dropped a glass water bowl. Of course, the commotion scared Bootsie even more, and he bolted away into the chilly dark.

Naturally, I could not rest without at least trying to help poor Bootsie find his way back home. So I cut Lucy's out time short, hustled her into the house, and gathered some things to help me entice a scared dog into my car, including two cans of chicken breast and a baggie of Milk-Bones. Then I raced out the door.

I trawled the neighborhood with my windows down, shining a flashlight between the dark houses of my warm and slumbering neighbors, and calling to Bootsie. Then I would see a flash of him, follow him, and try to talk softly to him. I even got out a few times, following him on foot, keeping him in my sight from a distance, kneeling in the grass, and waving drippy canned chicken in the air to make a fragrant trail for Bootsie to follow. A few times, he would appear interested and pace back and forth, but then he would bolt.

For nearly two hours Bootsie ran me and several other well-intentioned neighbors through the subdivision. Sadly, our efforts were in vain. Bootsie remained at large for nearly a week until he was caught. That little guy circled and circled for days, sleeping in his rescuer's garage at night and hiding during the day. He once was seen sleeping on a neighbor's screened porch. His rescuer set a trap, but he tripped it once without getting caught. He remained nearby all that time before finally tripping the trap with him inside of it. Bootsie is now safe, warm and fed. I only knew him a few days, but he left quite an impression on me. He will never know how much he has meant to me.

As I plodded afoot and/or drove around, I found myself muttering aloud, "C'mon, Boots. It's time to stop running…" or "Just stop running, buddy. There's a warm bed and food for you here with us." It was agony to know this poor, lost soul trusted nobody – not even the ones who offered food, shelter and comfort.

Then it occurred to me. I was just like Bootsie. That's what I was doing – running from God, bolting in the face of ongoing and relentless suffering. I had been waving my proverbial, feeble human fists in anger because of all the suffering I had endured and survived over even just the last four years. Wasn't it time for *me* to stop running and fall back on my faith, indeed to fall back on Him – my loving Father and Creator?

Over the years, I have researched techniques for catching a scared dog. The most successful approach is to never chase – just sit there calmly, always in view of the dog but not looking at him/her directly, rustle a plastic bag and eat (or pretend to eat) your bait of choice while making "num-num" sounds and licking your lips like dogs would when eating. Then you slowly build trust by "accidentally" dropping food and tossing bits of food in the dog's direction.

That was suddenly how I saw God. Here He was. He had never let me out of his sight. I just thought He had. I thought the good shepherd had completely forsaken this little lost lamb and was more concerned about his 99. I could not be more wrong.

God has been here the whole time, sitting calmly and patiently *at my level*, simply waiting for me to come to Him on my own when I was ready – by my choice – when I trusted Him. He keeps trying to show me good things, peace, and many graces despite all the suffering we humans inherited in this fallen world. I, like sweet Bootsie, simply must keep my eyes on Him and stop bolting and trying to figure it all out on my own when life overwhelms me. All that ever gets me is lost and further away from what I seek more than anything – the warmth and comfort of God's gentle promise of peace, hope, and love. Who else but a loving God and Father would lower himself to rescue and save me (or any human)? Who else would send his only son to do the same?

Until recently I was pretty good at finding the grace amid the suffering and trials of this life. Always I would look for the upside of every situation. There always is one. Even after my own cancer diagnosis and during treatment, I sought to find grace and humor and the good outcomes from an otherwise traumatic situation. In fact, my prayer immediately upon finding the lump was, *"Father, please. Let me handle whatever it ends up being with grace and humor, and let good come of it somewhere for someone – even if it's too late for me."* As always, God answered. Many good things came of that particular situation – deeper faith, courage, healing, stronger relationships, humor, laughter and fun in spite of it.

That was five years ago now. Since then, this world has thrown me an inordinate amount of trials and abject suffering. Truly...WAY too much... I seriously questioned that whole "God doesn't send you more than you can handle" thing. This feeble little human was at her limit. This feeble little human was feeling lost - like I was alone in a dinghy and simply drifting through endless, dense fog. Identifying the good outcomes and the glimmers of hope was not as easy or as immediate as it used to be.

At first, I thought (and was even told), *"Oh well. It is what it is. That's just life."* That only deepened the hopelessness. I was comforted and relieved when a Hospice grief counselor asserted that the events and losses of the last four years alone were *not* "just life," and that I have not had adequate time to recover from even one of those events before being bowled over by another traumatic loss, conflict, or major life change. I was truly ready to lie down and stay down. Yet despite my best attempts to do just that, I kept getting back up. That tells me God is not done with me yet.

This book is an attempt to answer His call to share my journey of faith through the most difficult times of my life. In fact, as I type, this world is testing my faith and especially my hope like never before. Yet I hold fast and dear to the knowledge that I am in the Lord's hands. I have praised him through other storms. I am tired, yes. I want to stop trying, yes. Yet then I think, *"Why stop now?"* So I, like little Bootsie, take a tentative step back toward the Lord.

Sometimes doubt creeps in, and I wonder why anyone would want to read about my experience and faith journey. Then I consider friends and others who are facing trials, traumas, and major life changes of their own. They apologize to me for their grief because they think "it's nothing like" what I am going through. The truth is…loss is loss. There is no comparing the type, size, quality or quantity of suffering. It simply hurts. This world hurts. Grief is our human response to that reality – and to our trials and suffering. If sharing my journey eases even one moment for someone else, this effort - this part of my own process - will not have been in vain.

Each of us has a unique response to grief and a different process and timeline for dealing with it. The beauty of God's promise assures us that He cares for us and that He is there for us through all of it. He knows what we need and when. He also offers us the body of Christ. As Christians, we have each other. We celebrate victories and graces. We hold each other up and encourage one another during difficult times. I pray that somehow the outcomes of my journey help others find hope and encouragement in the face of their grief, trials and suffering.

Heavenly Father and Christ Jesus, my Lord, I pray...

Thank you for giving me life. You are my Father. You are my rescuer. You know me inside and out. You are patient and gentle with me. You forgive me. You redeem me even when I bolt and wander away from you. Thank you for wee Bootsie and every other stray and lost soul we meet along this life's journey – both humans and creatures. All are special creations. They are gifts from a loving, gracious Father who wants us to come back to him and love him willingly, quietly and fully. Help me to learn from your example to be a quiet, gentle, patient servant to you and others.

In Jesus' name,
Amen

Chapter 2
The Hit List

Since, then, you have been raised with Christ, set
your heart on things above, where Christ is seated at the
right hand of God. Set your minds on things above, not on
earthly things. For you died, and your life is now hidden
with Christ in God.
– Colossians 3: 1-3 (NIV)

In my attempts to deal with all the loss and
suffering this world has inflicted upon me, I have turned
to a number of books about grief and grieving. Some
provided me with a kernel or two of helpful wisdom or
Scripture, but at the end of the day, those resources did
not reach me. At first I did not notice how most of them
focus on grief in response to death. Given where I was at
the time, it seemed appropriate that they focused on loss
due to death. That was, after all, the most significant loss I
had experienced. That was, after all, what I was enduring.

However, once I took the focus off of my own
suffering, such as when I tuned in to comfort a friend or
someone going through hardships, it hit me that loss is
about so much more than death. Loss is as varied as a
fingerprint – as are the many responses to it. Other major
life events can be seen as a type of loss and just as
traumatic – divorce, job changes, retirement, births,
graduation, moving to a new place...Even positive
changes are losses because they are the end of one chapter
and the start of a new one. In a way, they mark the death

of whatever preceded them. That is why I find myself comforting my comforters when they apologize for talking about grieving a loss because it is "nothing like" what I have experienced. I assure them that a loss is a loss and that my losses and suffering are no less or more significant than theirs.

Grief and loss do not follow a pattern or an orderly step-down program or progression. Grief and loss (and our responses to them) are spontaneous, unpredictable and downright ugly. My Hospice counselor described facing grief head-on as being down in the dirt, digging it up, churning it and truly working through it. I thought that was the perfect description of how I felt as I wrestled with my grief – tired, dirty, churning, frustrated, and (especially) lost and forsaken.

What I had not realized until that moment was how many losses I was grieving. It was not just losing David. I had lost so much more that was demanding to be grieved. It all started hitting me at once. The anxiety and tears would rise up out of nowhere and bowl me over – without warning and without solace – leaving me breathless and gasping for air. I was losing my faith and hope. Giving up was the one thing I had not tried.

Suffering and loss were not new to David. Nor are they new to me. Grieving it, however, is. Sometimes it saddens me that David never truly grieved his and our losses while he was here. His suffering just continued to the end. I find joy in now knowing that his worldly suffering has ended, and he can simply live in the light of the Lord's presence, grace and love.

God instructs us to think on good things. However, in order to put this conversation into the appropriate context, I have created what I affectionately call *The Hit List* – a chronicle of events leading up to this place and their cumulative effect. While David and I had experienced some losses in the seven years prior to the start of this list, it seemed like the world simply fell open in 2008.

The Hit List

2008

- We moved from our first home to a larger home with more maintenance.

- A merger at my then employer created a stressful and uncertain work environment. One result of the merger was a reduction in my years of service – from 10 years to none.

2009

- Our beloved Great Dane, Kittie, was diagnosed with bone cancer. After four months, she returned to Heaven.

- Stress-related illnesses and fibromyalgia

2010

- I left my employer after 12 years to obtain a Master's in Library Science.

- Our geriatric cat, Jeff, returned to Heaven.

- Close family members had serious health issues and multiple surgeries.

2011

- I found the lump in my breast. I had my first (and last) mammogram.

2012

- I was diagnosed with Stage 2 breast cancer which required six rounds of chemotherapy, a bilateral mastectomy, ongoing Herceptin (a targeted therapy) treatments thru January 2013, and five years of taking Tamoxifen (to prevent recurrence).

- Our little elderly Cocker Spaniel-Dachshund mix, Maggie, returned to Heaven.

- I underwent a bilateral mastectomy.

- Our stoic gentleman dog, Matrix, returned to Heaven (only 5 days after my surgery).

- I accepted my first school library job. After spending two weeks organizing and cleaning the place from top to bottom, I resigned.

- Compensation changes at David's employers further constricted our finances.

2013

- I was offered another school librarian job. I spent the entire summer cleaning out the media center only to resign shortly after school began.

- My dad passed away.

- David started spending hours alone after work and thousands of dollars at sports bars.

2014

- David confided to me that he thought he had a drinking problem.

- On December 1, David was diagnosed with Stage 4 metastatic pancreatic and liver cancer. His prognosis was one year and a couple weeks.

- David started a blistering series of chemo blasts which ended up being too much for him.

- Around Christmas, at the urging of a close family member, one of David's ex-girlfriends started trying to reconnect with him. This had a profoundly negative impact on his health.

2015

- In January, we switched David to my oncologist to begin a different chemo regimen.

- Little old Sidney, our sweet, shy 20-year-old gray cat, returned to Heaven.

- In March, Tillman, our Great Dane, was diagnosed with bone cancer.

- David tried to stop the communication with his high school girlfriend, which resulted in a restraining order against a close family member.

- I started a new job as the school librarian at the best school in the universe – Lewisville

Elementary School. I spent the entire summer cleaning out yet another media center.

- We had Tillman's rear left leg amputated to alleviate his pain and discomfort.

2016

- On February 9 (the day before David's last birthday), my Tillman returned to Heaven.

- March 21: Sweet, gentle David flew to his beloved Jesus and returned to Heaven.

- March 22 – October: The rest of 2016 was a blur and a flurry of events and major changes.

  - Renewing the restraining order
  - Moving myself and our two dogs to a new home
  - Listing the house David and I had shared
  - Maintaining two houses
  - Starting a new school year with a new boss and a longer commute
  - Looking for a new job and losing my loving, supportive school family

Heavenly Father and Christ Jesus, my Lord, I pray...

Thank you for raising me with Christ. You promise unconditional love and acceptance even when I let this life's trials and setbacks distract me from your loving arms. Thank you for not abandoning me. Thank you for keeping me in your sights and gently reminding me of your presence and your all-encompassing love. May I learn to understand and accept that obstacles are gifts that will strengthen my heart, my faith and my ability to be one of your lights to others in this fallen world. May I learn to appreciate trials and suffering instead of fearing or dreading them. May I willingly and quietly accept your yoke and follow wherever your gentle hand leads me.

In Jesus' name,
Amen

Chapter 3
The Day the World Fell Open

*There is a time for everything, and a season for every
activity under heaven.*
- Ecclesiastes 3:1 (NIV)

*Then Jesus said to his disciples: "Therefore I tell you, do
not worry about your life...Who of you by worrying can
add a single hour to his life? Since you cannot do this
very little thing, why do you worry about the rest?"*
- Luke 12:22, 25-26

David and I met in 1999 when I moved into my
first little apartment. We often passed each other in the
parking lot, smiled and sometimes waved - as civilized
strangers do. Finally, one day he got up the nerve to ask
me out. His pick-up line was, "Would you like to go get
coffee sometime?" The fact that neither of us drank coffee
was irrelevant. We learned later on that when he asked,
we both were thinking about non-coffee drinks. I thought,
"I'll just drink tea." He was thinking, "I'll have Coke."
And so it began.

We were married in 2000 in a small ceremony on
a perfect September evening in a tiny old chapel that used
to belong to an orphanage. We could not have asked for a
more perfect start to our life together if we had requested
a Hollywood script: The weather was perfect – clear, star-
lit, and the perfect temperature. We had picked the most

perfect weekend because the weather presented a challenge on the Saturdays before and after our big day. All of the important people in our lives were there except for David's best friend. My five-year-old nephew decided to stick to the script and *not* run out of the church to go look at the military wall of honor instead of fulfilling his duties as our ring-bearer (like he did during rehearsal). Our guests relaxed, danced and enjoyed themselves at the reception which was held in a pink, antique Victorian house. What more could we have asked for?

David looked so handsome in his tux. He was a comfortably large guy even after losing some pre-wedding weight. Despite a taste for beer, BBQ and French fries, he was healthy and health conscious – always taking vitamin supplements and keeping abreast of health news. He also was an expert hugger and foot rubber. He was a hesitant smiler who rarely showed his teeth because of some damage from a very high childhood fever. Yet at our wedding he wore a huge, handsome grin. He looked so happy and proud. I used to tease him that he never smiled ever again as big as he did at our wedding.

We bought our first home in 2001. It was tract-built home in a subdivision of postage-stamp sized lots, but to us it was home – and it was perfect for us. It was comfortable, just the right size and on a private lot surrounded by trees in the back and a common area with trees on one side. The pale-yellow siding and green shutters and front door always made me smile. I painted and decorated every single room. I planted roses, dwarf daylilies and other flowers, and I stacked a zillion bags worth of river rock around every bed. David was proud of the Chinese Pistache tree he chose for the back yard. A menagerie of wildlife - deer, rabbits, birds of every kind and color, and an occasional possum – made their homes in our yard. You could not even see the massive power tower trail behind the rear hill. We were both so proud of that place. David was especially proud because he happened to have enough cash at the time to hold the premium lot on which the house would be built.

By 2008, the once quiet neighborhood had mushroomed into hundreds of homes and an additional swimming pool and recreation center. Needless to say, it had gotten noisy. We still loved our little haven, but the once unoccupied common area next to our home became the center of every child's (and every dog's) attention. Cut-through foot traffic and speeding increased. It was getting more difficult to enjoy our little slice of paradise. So…We started looking elsewhere.

We had always enjoyed small towns and envied those who lived close enough to walk to restaurants and town events like parades and art festivals. David suggested we look at Waxhaw, and he happened to find two houses within walking distance of the historic downtown and what would become our favorite restaurants and walking paths. As luck would have it, the company that built the new homes we visited also owned rental properties. We basically swapped houses, thereby avoiding the traditional realtor process. We thought we had hit the jackpot, and we praised God because everything seemed to work out in our favor.

We bade farewell to our sweet little house and moved to the new, larger home with more maintenance and other costs. Of course, we closed on the house about three minutes before the worst real estate crash in decades. So our new home's value was way underwater even before we turned the key as owners. In addition to unexpected up-front expenses and declining values of the new home, we also had to repair the air conditioner at the other house. What made the move more difficult was how much we had loved our other home. We had worked so hard to make it cozy and to make it ours. We regretted letting our little haven get turned into a rental property. We were attached to it, but we had foolishly (we thought at that point) let it go. We instantly regretted moving. The new home was beautiful. It was unique and special. Yet it felt cursed. We felt cursed. We felt sharp pangs of regret and loss. It took us over a year to feel settled enough to start enjoying and loving our new home. We could not have known how short-lived our newly blossoming appreciation would be.

The Static

When we moved to our new home, David and I were both enjoying the fruits of our work-life labors. We were both making enough money to support our new home, even though sometimes the budget got tight. A few years would pass before we figured out why that was, but for now we were content with our paychecks and overall lifestyle. We praised God for the blessings. We felt him smiling on us, and we eventually seemed settled. We soon learned the hard way to be cautiously optimistic and never completely settled because life can change on a dime.

I worked in a corporate pressure cooker. There is no graceful way of saying that. The latest corporate merger at my then employer created a stressful and uncertain work environment. The first impact of the merger on me was a reduction in my years of service – from 10 years to none – due to a human resources policy change. Everyone was on edge about their jobs. My co-workers were vying for fewer positions, even tearing each other down in order to secure their jobs. I suddenly hated my job, and I started to lose faith in the human race. I felt insignificant, replaceable, and useless. My workplace frustration and hopelessness carried over to my home life. I felt trapped and chained to a certain paycheck in order to pull my fair share and then some.

At that time, I earned more than David so I felt especially responsible for maintaining a certain income, but it came at a cost. I was plagued by anxiety and stress-related illnesses, ongoing pain and fatigue due to the merger and a newly hostile work environment. I once jumped straight up in the middle of the night from a deep sleep, out of bed, gasping for air. We almost called 911 because I could not catch my breath. The doctor diagnosed me with Fibromyalgia. Little did we know that was the least of the challenges we faced.

Kittie

Kittie was a sweet, gentle Great Dane – a noble, sleek black creation from God himself indeed. She was 130 pounds of love and submissive gentleness. I found her through a post on an employee bulletin board in 2001. "Free," it read. I could not dial the phone fast enough. First I called the person who was parting with Kittie to get information and set up a time to meet her. Then I called David. We already had a sassy little Cocker Spaniel-Dachshund mix, Maggie, whom we had rescued from the countryside a couple years before. David, naturally, agreed to the new (albeit large) addition to our pack, and once again we praised God for another happy circumstance. I sent Kittie's picture to all our friends, one of whom unfairly commented that she looked like a cross-eyed pony. I didn't care. I loved Kittie. However, had social media been around then, I may have un-friended the person who made that comment (even though it was meant in good fun).

Kittie adored children and pizza. Whenever the two combined, Kittie was especially pleased because she always managed to steal a slice or two from the unsuspecting little human. In fact, when we met her for the first time she was working the dinner table. The woman's little girl sat at the table, not minding where her slice of pizza was. Kittie, meanwhile, was circling like a shark wearing a cloaking device. The little girl and her pizza never saw Kittie coming. I knew immediately that Kittie would fit right in. At first she was extremely shy and scared of everything – especially men, leashes, and ceiling fans – but she eventually settled in just fine.

Kittie kept us laughing. She sampled a windowsill, remote controls, frames, picture easels. She left holes in the stairwell wall at our first home while barreling down the steps with Maggie (a.k.a. Little M and Booglet). Little M could maneuver like a cat. Kittie, however, cornered more like a Mack truck. That was okay. We just laughed, patched up the drywall and moved on. She dragged me through the backyard to the fence so she could touch noses with another dog. Life with a Great Dane! We would not have traded it for anything.

Kittie had no idea what a protector she was. Her big girl bark and leggy presence at the front door once scared the UPS guy into leaving the package at the end of the sidewalk. The cable guy (who resembled Mr. Clean and Robo-Cop) caught sight of Kittie peering down from the top landing where she stood behind a baby gate. He said something about "that gorilla up there," and Kittie barked only once. I have never seen someone so large move so fast. His feet sprouted booster jets, and he bolted for the bonus room and slammed the door shut. I could hear him behind the door on the phone telling someone about "the biggest dog." I had to giggle and give Kittie a smooch on her head. That was only fair. After all, he had called her a gorilla.

One of the reasons we liked our new home so much was the larger yard and brand new privacy fence. Kittie enjoyed her new kingdom. She loved to lie in the sun and just bake. She could hunker down and peer through the gap in the back gate to watch the deer. She probably wondered why they never came over to her – perhaps the same reason the cable guy's feet sprouted wings. She could look pretty intimidating.

Nine months had passed in the new house when yet another maelstrom hit. We noticed a knot on Kittie's front right leg and took her to the vet. Our beloved 9 ½ year old Kittie angel was diagnosed with bone cancer. The vet told us just to love her and give her anything she wanted. Given Kittie's age, he did not recommend amputation. Kittie was so brave and sweet. She hung on and enjoyed her specially cooked meals of chicken and rice and cheese and lots of extra cookies. She figured out how to hold her front leg up to scurry around and climb on the couch and bed. She just adapted and rolled on with living the time she had left. She never asked about when or what if. She just lived each day as it came. Her adaptability and courage were amazing and humbling to witness.

After four months, her leg tumor had nowhere else to go. It broke open, leaving her leg a mangled mess. We had wrapped it, but that did not help. She went out that morning, did her business, came in, and rested on the hard floor – something she never did. Then she stopped eating even her cookies. She never got back up. We knew it was time. We had to help her return to Heaven. It was my honor to be holding her when she transitioned to the Rainbow Bridge.

Kittie and Justin

Where was God?

After Kittie left us, I was heartbroken and numb. I felt guilty for not being able to ease her suffering at the end. Even though I knew she told us when she was ready, I worried that we had waited too long. Maybe we should have had her leg amputated early on. Had we given her enough pain meds? Did I spend enough time with her? I should not have gotten impatient with her for barking. I did not comfort her enough. Did she know how much we loved her? Such thoughts roiled around my brain and tore at my heart to the point where I could not sleep. I would breakdown and cry at the sight of her Scooby blankets. I bawled when we had to throw her giant round bed away. Once we even thought we heard her bark.

Our other little dog, Maggie, even "saw" Kittie. We heard the sound of dog tags clinking together like they do when a dog shakes vigorously. We knew it was not Maggie's or Matrix's because they were right in front of us. Then suddenly Maggie stood up and marched to the edge of the bed with her tail up and wagging, looking down like she used to do when Kittie would stand beside the bed. She stood like that for a minute and then resumed her previous position. It was a momentary encounter, but David and I both had goose bumps afterwards.

I am not a mystic by any means, but I do find dreams absolutely fascinating. They can terrorize and comfort – sometimes even in the same dream. I find comfort in dreams when I consider their timing and messages. I believe God uses them to communicate with us. He sent such a dream to me shortly after Kittie died. I believe He wanted to ease my heart and mind.

In the dream, I was escorting an elderly woman across the street. By the time we reached the other side, the woman was morphing into a sweet lady who had lived with my family after her husband passed away. As she sat she said, "Thank you for all you did in my life." As she finished speaking, she morphed into Kittie. Suddenly there was my angel girl! I hugged her and buried my face in her neck, simply bawling.

Whenever Kittie wanted our attention or a cookie, she would reach out her leg and paw in what I called her "ballet move" – a long and graceful, slow motion of drawing her paw toward herself. That's just what she did now – stretching her long, graceful leg in her little ballet move – multiple times. She was telling me she was okay and thanking me for all we had done to help her – that she was safe and happy – and that her leg was whole and perfect again (no more giant, mangled tumor). I cried when I woke up from that one. At the same time, I felt a new sense of peace about Kittie. I still missed her, of course, but I was no longer churning over what I should have-would have-could have-didn't do. I stopped beating myself up – about that particular situation at least.

What Else?

I am not a fan of that question, "What else?" because invariably something else happens. For that very reason, I do not even utter it anymore. I do not need to. The difficulties and traumas just keep rolling in. I was informed by many that hardship and trauma were "just life." So I simply accepted it – often with frustration and anger, but I nonetheless just moved ahead through whatever came our way.

My favorite line from *Gone with the Wind* is one in which Scarlett's grandmother said of her, "You don't make a fuss about things that can't be helped even if they are disagreeable. You take your fences cleanly like a good hunter."[1] Looking at my copy of that classic novel now, I see where I marked it – in ink. I remember aspiring to have someone describe me in such a complimentary way. I wanted to "take my fences cleanly." I got my chance.

By 2010, my work challenges had mounted into what was an insurmountable mountain chain of frustration, anger, and never feeling that I would measure up and get anything right. Being displaced and without a paycheck was a 24/7 worry. As usual, David adopted his instinctive, supportive, problem-solving stance. Both of us churned, prayed and talked at length about the implications of my leaving the corporate world and transitioning to a career in education, specifically to be an elementary school librarian. I loved kids and books and school. It sounded like a perfect match.

So, I yanked off the Band-Aid and left my employer after a 12-year career to pursue a Master's in Library Science. I also had gotten into law school, but I chose Library Science and kids over law school - a fact I have used as a club to beat myself up by throwing it back in my own face and even regretting many times since. I also felt guilty because returning to school full- time created an income gap that David was able to make up only by working extra hours. Once again, all I could see was that a positive change that was supposed to improve our situation and happiness only exacerbated things. I was starting to feel like I had a special gift for making things worse. Still we moved ahead as planned. We chose to trust in the Lord, but we did not see the other fences until they were upon us.

The Obstacle Course

While David worked, I attended school and maintained the house and yard in order to take some of the load off of David. At the same time, several close family members suffered from serious health issues and several surgeries. We had heard from my sisters that my father was in and out of hospitals for one ailment or another. His care was becoming too much for my mother to manage. David, the constant worrier and protector, helped with as much as he could. He wanted to take time off to help everyone, but he was unable to do so. He was always on the road.

Our four-legged companions were not exempt from the suffering. Our geriatric cat, Jeff, had to be put down due to age-related issues at 21 years old. He had been a faithful, comforting companion for David prior to our marriage. He saw David through some very tough times. Now he was gone. I had to take him to the vet by myself because David was on the road and too far away to get home in time.

I was never a cat person until David's two cats came into my life. Despite my attempts to *not* be a cat person, Jeff and Sidney won me over. They were quite a pair. Jeff was a sturdy - overweight – tabby. Sidney was a sweet tiny, gray and furry boy who squeaked instead of meowing, which earned him the nickname "Peepers." Gentle David had adopted both of them from an ASPCA group in Virginia. Jeff had been in a cat colony in a state prison. He had a clipped ear to prove it. Sidney was found in a dumpster in the snow as a kitten. Jeff and Sidney had been faithful companions and comforts for David through a difficult breakup and job change and his move to North

Carolina. He often talked about how they would meet him at the door and keep him warm at night by sleeping on the covers between his legs and around his head. Now one of them was taking his leave without David by his side. David and I were both heart-broken.

Some insist that one's animals are "just" that – animals, as if they are somehow less important than humans. However, to us, our pets are our family. They are our companions – our friends. David and I both accepted that and loved them as such. Our pets teach us how to develop love, patience, selflessness, and humor - among many other things. They are gifts from God himself indeed. Whenever we watched the news or saw some other situation that caused us to lose faith in the human race, we would puzzle about why God put humans above animals in this world. We both firmly believed that our animals will meet us when we reach our heavenly reward. This love, while a gift, makes losing our pets that much more traumatic and painful.

Once again, we did what God asked of us - trying, not always successfully, to do so without complaint or anger. David and I accepted the outcomes of each day and looked ahead to the next day. We still took our fences cleanly, but it was getting more difficult to propel ourselves forward, up and over. Good thing our ears were up and we were watching where we were going.

Heavenly Father and Christ Jesus, my Lord, I pray...

Thank you for inviting me to be your child. May I always find joy in knowing that I am wholly yours, that I am a child of the risen Lord who conquered the grave. May I always know that you loved me enough to send your only son to suffer mercilessly and die for me. Make me ever-mindful that no matter what trials I face in this life, they do not mark the end of my world. Help me to always know that the worst thing that could happen to me is to not be accepted into Heaven. Help me to live my life according to your word. Help me develop a heart of gratitude for my life and all of its moments – both the good and the difficult ones.

In Jesus' name,
Amen

Chapter 4
Arming for Battle

*Therefore, as God's chosen people, holy and
dearly loved, clothe yourselves with compassion,
kindness, humility, gentleness and patience... And over all
these virtues put on love, which binds them all together in
perfect unity.*
– Colossians 3: 12-14 (NIV)

*You armed me with strength for battle; you made my
adversaries bow at my feet.*
- 2 Samuel 22:40 (NIV)

*And my God will meet all your needs according to
the riches of his glory in Christ Jesus.*
- Philippians 4:19 (NIV)

David was a gift from God to this world. He was a
wonderful man – the kindest and best of men, in fact. He
was not overly demonstrative or affectionate. He was a
large, stoic and gentle man with a giant heart of service.
As a counselor, his first instinct was to protect and always
put others first. Most of all, David loved Jesus. He lived
his life each day in response to the question, *what would
Jesus do?*

Was he perfect? No. Did he have moments of doubt? Of course he did. Did he get angry at the abject cruelty of this world? Sure. Yet David's was a deep, quiet and unswerving faith. Through example and quiet testimony, he sought to share that faith with others and always sought opportunities to bring others closer to Jesus. I was humbled by his quiet obedience. I sought to be obedient to God, but sometimes (depending on what was being asked of me), I would ask questions, drag my feet, and pitch a fit before I fell in line. David's obedience was consistently quiet and soft. I admired him for that.

In 2011, I got my chance to respond as David would – quietly, easily, without challenging or questioning. It was a December evening. David was not home yet. I was cleaning the house and had stopped to stretch. I was stretching my shoulders with my arms folded up and my hands over my chest like I had wings. I stretched and let my hands fall. As they drifted back down, they ran across my chest. That's when I felt it – a hard knot on my right breast. I knew from our experience with Kittie's hard knot what it meant. I knew immediately what it was.

Susan Boyle's elegantly sweet voice happened to be singing "Make Me a Channel of Your Peace."[ii] Instantly I hit my knees and prayed, *"Please, just let me handle whatever it is with grace and humor, and let some good come of it somewhere for someone – even if it's not for me."* I felt instant and true peace – the peace that surpasses all understanding. I repeated my prayer and stayed on my knees for a few more moments to breathe deeply. I stood up. Then I wrote myself a sticky note to schedule my first (and last) mammogram.

The Armor

The results of my mammogram required additional diagnostic tests, including an ultrasound. I focused on the fact that not all lumps were cancer and tried to focus on each moment at hand instead of running off down the road assuming anything, especially without adequate information. I sat in the imaging office alone, watching couples as they waited to be escorted back to see the doctor or get their tests done. Part of me wondered if I should have asked David to join me. Then I shook that off and tried to read a magazine.

When it was my turn, they took me back to a dimly lit room and asked me to disrobe. I instantly felt small, helpless and alone. Suddenly the room felt cold, but I did as instructed and laid back on the table and closed my eyes, enjoying the quiet hum of the machines and the dark room. I started to relax. The ultrasound went smoothly. The technician remained quietly cheerful. So, I relaxed again. Then the radiologist came in to discuss the results. She was kind but reserved and oddly quiet – almost cold. I could feel a tension or something. I knew. I did. I felt it. Yet once again I shoved that aside and focused on the moment. I asked her what she was seeing. She never showed me the screen, but she said something about the elongated shape of the lump. She said a biopsy would be needed, and that she would see about getting it scheduled. Then she left the room. That was it. I started to cry. I felt so cut off.

When the tech came back in, she informed me that the biopsy was scheduled for a few days later. I objected, almost starting to cry again, and asked if there was any way we could get it done sooner. In a shaky voice, I told her it was not really fair to say such things and make someone wait for days to even have the test run. She stepped out, and the next thing I know, the radiologist came back in with her, ready to do the biopsy. She said she had an opening. Looking back, I think she gave up her lunch hour because it was 12:30. I thanked the radiologist for fast-tracking my tests. She was suddenly much friendlier. And so began my journey.

In January 2012, David and I sat quietly in the waiting room of the imaging center's office. The biopsy results had come in. At one point the nurse receptionist ushered us into a room by ourselves. That was probably red flag number one, but we did not dwell on that. We also saw a large paperback workbook about breast cancer on a credenza. Yes, I wondered if it was mine. In my heart, I knew it was. Yet we waited.

I did not recognize the radiologist who delivered the news. She was very kind and soft-spoken. She came in with another nurse who I would learn later was my Nurse Navigator. We got through the pleasantries and introductions and information about the tests. Finally, she said simply, "It's cancer." David reached for my hand. He had tears in his eyes. I did not. I refused to cry – especially if he was going to cry. What a mess we would be! I simply squeezed his hand and turned my eyes to the doctor.

When I heard the word officially, I actually was relieved. The pink elephant in the room was now visible. My next reaction was frustration. *This is so not convenient*, I thought. I was in the last semester of my Masters of Library Science program. Our finances were tight. How were we going to afford the out-of-pocket costs? I took a short breath and kind of let it out in a huff.

I think the doctor thought I was crying. I think she expected me to fall to pieces, but I did not. Instead I asked her point-blank, "So what's next? When do we get started?"

My Nurse Navigator took the reins then and explained the next steps: a breast MRI, pathology tests to determine type, staging and treatment plans as well as CT scans to make sure the cancer had not spread elsewhere, as well as meeting with a surgeon and getting a port installed. It was quite a list of unknowns, tests and procedures.

I think I surprised them when I asked if the surgeon had any openings that day. I was ready to start checking things off my list and getting this behind us – whatever it was. Once again, they fast-tracked us and got us over to the surgeon that afternoon. It was a premature meeting, of course, because we still did not have all of the details needed to make decisions, but it helped us feel like we were getting started. We at least could start considering options. Later that evening, I created a spreadsheet and a project plan of options and dates. I called it "Project Pink." We were off.

It would be a week before we knew what we were facing. It was a week before I knew my prognosis. As always, the not-knowing was worse than knowing. Other than lots of reading, making lists of to-do questions, researching and churning of "What ifs" and endlessly roiling questions, I could not tell you anything about that week of waiting – and trying *not* to wonder.

Answers

A week or so later we learned my cancer was localized, Stage 2, and the type that required six rounds of a chemotherapy regimen known as TCH: two traditional chemotherapy agents - Taxotere and Carboplatin - and a targeted treatment called Herceptin. I received six rounds of all three agents from January through May. In between those treatments, I had weekly infusions of Herceptin until January 2013. I also had to take Tamoxifen for five years.

When I first saw the chemo room and other patients who appeared weak and sleeping and discolored, it occurred to me, "I'm sick." Instantly, something in me revolted. Instantly, I banished that thought and refused to be sick. Never would I use that word again during or after treatment. I still will not refer to myself or that time in my life as "when I was sick." Always I say, "When I was going through treatment." Somehow that made a difference.

What We Need and When

As always, God appears when we need him and when we openly receive him and appreciate the moment. While we waited for our tour of the chemo room and the process, I sat down in one of the large recliners next to a gentle woman named Mary who was there for her breast cancer treatment, which turned out to be the same regimen as mine. She touched my hand and looked right into my deer-in-the-headlights eyes, comforting me and telling me I was going to be okay. "The worst part is the fatigue," she said. "Don't worry. You'll be all right. I promise." Her words touched my heart so gently that I could only thank her quietly and push back the tears that had started to appear. Her quiet strength and comforting presence allowed me to joke with the nurses about changing my treatment day so I could be there the same day as Mary. After that, it was all good. I think I only saw Mary one other time after that, but I will never forget her. At that moment, she was one of God's finest angels.

Before and during treatment I also spoke with other women who were going through treatment or were survivors. It seemed like everyone we met either knew someone who had gone through cancer treatment or had gone through it themselves. The volunteer at the Buddy Kemp House hat and scarf "boutique" was a survivor. Survivors, patients and relatives were in every waiting room and every store or restaurant – a fact that made me stop and think that we never know what other people are going through at any given time. I vowed then to be more aware of others and where they might be at that moment. I wanted them to see God's grace and Jesus' example through me.

I also wanted to be to someone else what Mary and others had been for me. I wanted to be an example of grace under pressure. I wanted to laugh *in spite of* (never *at*) cancer. I wanted to show others that there is life during and after cancer – even if the outcome is not the desired one. I wanted to wear that "Survivor" tee shirt. More than anything, I wanted to make God smile. I wanted Jesus to tell me one day that I had been a "good and faithful servant."

The Battle Plan

I quickly learned that not only is it acceptable, it is necessary, to question our doctors. By questioning, I don't mean questioning their knowledge or wondering if they know what they're doing or their course of action. I mean asking questions to learn – to educate ourselves – and truly understand what is happening. I wanted to know everything I could about my diagnosis and treatment so I would make informed choices. For example, the typical initial recommendation for women with my diagnosis and type of cancer is a lumpectomy or single mastectomy with reconstruction and radiation. Doctors try to follow the least invasive course of action. I get that. I do. As far as I was concerned, however, I had already been invaded, and I wanted the interloper gone – all gone. I did not want to be like the women we met who were going back through surgery and/or chemo because they had opted for the recommended course of treatment. I was taking no chances. My stubborn streak paid off for once.

My breast MRI uncovered a tiny suspicious dot on the left breast. Immediately, I said, "We're done. Bilateral mastectomy." No questions. No more discussion. The recommended surgery path was the mastectomy, then a surgery to install expanders, wait a few months to gradually fill and tweak those, then have another surgery to install the final silicone implants. I weighed all the options. Then I held up the STOP sign. I even considered not having reconstruction and talked to a prosthetics company about falsies. I was serious until I realized how it worked. Then I laughed. I already had to put contacts in my eyes every day. Picking the right prosthetic and stuffing my bra every day just sounded like more work than I wanted.

A wonderful co-worker of David's happened to just be finishing her cancer journey as I was starting mine. She told me about a "direct to implant" procedure which would allow me to have implants installed during the first surgery. I also opted for saline (a more natural material) instead of silicone. Researching my options allowed me to make the best choices for me. I had to live with my choices for a long time. I also wanted to be done with doctors by that point. I wanted nothing that would pose another health hazard or require additional, ongoing monitoring. Having a say in my treatment and plan and making decisions that worked for me took some effort and a great deal of time, but it helped me feel more confident during and after treatment. I may not have had control of the situation. That belonged to God. But I did have a say.

Finding Grace and Good

Before I could be an example, I had to learn from example. Once again, the Lord crossed my path with someone who would make a lasting impact on me that he would never know. This particular gentleman was a complete stranger. I never even met him. I hope someday God will give me the opportunity to thank him. For now, I'll call him Harry.

It was the day of my first treatment. As promised, God met me there. It was a warm, sunny day for January. My first treatment went smoothly. David worked on his laptop while I lounged in a recliner for nearly four hours. I think I even may have slept a little. I was hesitant to eat much until I knew if/when/how the chemo would affect my stomach, but I snacked on some crackers and soda. Luckily, I never had any issues with nausea. I just tried to eat light meals in the first few days after each treatment.

David had to meet a client at a nearby library right after my treatment. So I tagged along. Because it was so nice, I stayed in the car while David went inside. I rolled down the windows, closed my eyes and just relaxed. As I sunned myself like a cat in the sun, I heard voices that brought me out of my fog. On his way in to the library, Harry was flagging down a younger gentleman walking in the opposite direction. He hailed the young man with, "Hey, young man! Have you made your New Year's resolutions yet?" The young guy appeared as confused as I was. I rolled my eyes to myself and muttered, "This oughta' be good." Boy, was it ever. As always, it was just what I needed to hear.

Harry explained to the young man that he was retired from United States Army after over 30 years. "And what I learned," he said with extra gusto, "was to expect nothing and appreciate everything! So that egg I ate this morning was a new egg for a new day!" My eyes stopped rolling, and I was instantly humbled.

What I learned in that moment not only re-set my perspective about my treatment and the outcomes (which at that point I did not know). It re-set my perspective on life. I took his words to mean that I should not anticipate things - that I should just roll with whatever came. I stopped churning and wondering – and started simply accepting. Later I chuckled a bit because I felt that God was slapping me upside the back of the head and saying, "If you're gonna' eavesdrop, then pay attention, kiddo! This one's for you." *Thank you, God.*

And thank you, Harry. Thanks to you, I developed a stronger, more positive attitude that has infused everything I do. I try to live up to your example every day.

I was bald and in menopause at 42, but I discovered a stronger sense of humor in spite of an otherwise trying time. I bought and hung a "Tiki Bar" sign on my chemo pole which always got a few smiles and even a couple chuckles when I pulled that out of my bag and hung it up. It had little "Closed" and "Open" tags on it which I flipped to "Closed" whenever I took a nap. I bought fun tee shirts to wear after surgery. I also drank more water than any one person should (110 ounces one day). Because I stayed so hydrated, I was able to do yard work and spread bales of pine needles even after my fourth treatment. Then somewhere between treatments four and five, I actually could feel that the lump had shrunk. It was dissolving! That just fueled my fire to check off each treatment and stage of this battle. I was actually happy just rolling with things as they came. How liberating! I also now have a great collection of hats.

Yes, I felt pretty beaten up physically by the end of my treatment. Mary was right. The fatigue was the worst part – until I had to live with 4 post-surgical drains for almost a month. *Yuck* - and what a pain, but I survived. Yes, I survived! *Thank you, God.*

Heavenly Father and Christ Jesus, my Lord, I pray...

Thank you for your quiet, healing hand. It is to you alone I owe my gratitude for you provided for my every need. You crossed my path with many angels who brought comfort, healing, and humor during even the most challenging times. You calmed me. You answered. Thank you for the image of lying at the foot of the cross with Jesus' arms around me. That image comforted me through even the dark of night and days of uncertainty. You answered in your time. You smiled on me and brought me through the flames and the most treacherous waters. Thank you for not being done with me yet. May I make you proud as I live out the rest of my days here and into eternity.

In Jesus' name,
Amen

Chapter 5
Scuffs on the Armor

*The Lord is close to the brokenhearted and saves
those who are crushed in spirit. A righteous man may
have many troubles, but the Lord delivers him from them
all; he protects all his bones, not one of them will be
broken.*
– Psalm 34:18-20 (NIV)

*The Lord builds up Jerusalem; he gathers the
exiles of Israel. He heals the brokenhearted and binds up
their wounds.*
- Psalm 147:3 (NIV)

David always said that everything would work out
– even when we did not have all the answers. His faith
was simple and sturdy. Just as God placed Harry in my
path at the perfect time, He also knew when to ask us to
clear a few more fences. At the time, we did not
appreciate them, but once over them, we realized they
were part of strengthening us and reinforcing our faith for
greater battles yet to come. I suppose God figured if our
armor did not have a few chinks and scuffs in it, we
would be ill-prepared. As usual, He was right. At the
time, it did not feel like it, but He was.

One particularly difficult skirmish erupted
shortly after I graduated from chemo. Our little elderly
Cocker Spaniel-Dachshund mix, Maggie, had started
having unexplained seizures. Once after my fourth chemo

treatment, I thought we had lost her to one of them. She had fallen off the bed during a seizure and just lay on the floor, seemingly lifeless. I knelt over her and buried my face in her soft ears, begging her not to leave me. Not now. I cried. I begged God to spare her, and that if He was going to take her, to just do it quickly, softly and with no pain. Maggie groggily roused herself out of the post-seizure fog and returned to her normal sassy self – a little more tired and slower, but still quite intact. I praised God and thanked him for the special and generous gift of Maggie and her recovery. *Another reprieve,* I thought.

Maggie (aka Little M.) was my special little friend. She was an adorably sassy, golden thing who took no guff from anyone – one of the traits I admired most about her. In her mind and heart, she was a Rottweiler.

David and I were visiting my parents one day in 1999 when a little blur of gold zipped around us as fast as her little legs would go. We laughed and laughed. Maggie had chosen us. David and I were still just dating, so Maggie became my little companion. I loved her dearly. We had so many late-night chats and snuggles. I told her all of my secrets. She told me nothing. She did, however, teach me a lot about how important humor, patience, and calculated mischief were to one's well-being and survival. It was the first time I had a dog of my very own, and I adored her.

Unfortunately, Maggie would experience another seizure a few weeks before my bilateral mastectomy. My little M. returned to Heaven at 13 years old after suffering from another seizure. We found her in our closet early one morning. She had crossed over during the night. She was gone before I could tell her I loved her. I berated myself for not hearing her and for not being there with her as she slipped away. I wrapped her up in one of her blankets, covered my bald head and drove Little M.'s body to the vet by myself. I talked to her the whole way and told her I loved her. Her passing was just weeks before my bilateral mastectomy. I was devastated. I had lost one of my great comforts in the world. My lights dimmed just a bit, and I think I nicked the top of this particular fence. Yet on I went.

Maggie

Angel Dog and Hero

We always called Matrix our guardian. He was a handsome, Bull Terrier/Border Collie/Lab mix with two striking blue eyes that reflected the purest heart. He was always sturdy, always steady. He also found my breast cancer years before my first (and last) mammogram. One night in 2007, I was settling into bed when Matrix suddenly jumped up on the bed and honed right in on my right breast. His nose was like a magnet. He wouldn't leave the spot alone. I should have paid attention because in December 2011 I found the lump right where Matrix had so insistently examined all those years before.

Matrix, ever watchful, also stood guard over me the night of the diagnosis. I was restless and slept in spurts because of all the questions churning in my mind. Matrix knew. He normally slept on the bed at our feet. That night, however, he slept at the head of the bed. He stood watch, keeping a paw on me all night. Whenever I woke up, he was there - asleep with his head on mine or just lying there awake and watching over me. It was beautiful.

Matrix also was his usual guardian self throughout my chemo, treatment, and all the decisions. He always knew what to do, what we needed, and when. He was always there for us. He saw us through it all. Then, less than one week after my double mastectomy, Matrix unexpectedly went back to Heaven. We had laid down for a nap together, but he woke up with God. I found him lying in his usual napping position on the couch. He left us like he had lived - gently and stoically.

Matrix was only 11 years old, and now his stunning blue eyes were closed to us forever. This unexpected blow came less than one week *after* my bilateral mastectomy. That morning we had played "Connect the Dots" like we did every day. Matrix would get playful, rolling over on his back and wriggling around with his legs flailing with all the silliness he could muster. Then one of us would rub his Butterball chest and stomach vigorously and give extra scratches to the five black dots on his otherwise pure white stomach and chest.

Matrix's passing was especially hard on David

because he and Matrix were like peas and carrots. Matrix had come so far and learned to trust. I guess he taught that to us, too. We both sorely missed his gentle spirit. Matrix is an angel from God himself. He always was. I am so honored to have been one of his people - to have loved him here, and to know that we get to love him forever when we are all reunited in Heaven.

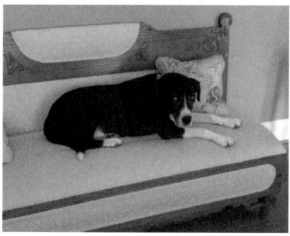

Matrix – Our Sturdy Guardian

Exits Only – No Rest Stops

Although yet another part of our hearts had
stopped beating when Matrix returned to Heaven, we
knew life marched on. We tried to find the good moments
in this world. At this point, however, we felt that
somehow they were not as accessible or frequent. I think
we were both getting so worn down that we simply did
not notice them as readily.

I was just two months out from my surgery and
still wearing hats to cover my stubbly hair when I was
offered my first school library job. I thought I was ready.
After months of praying and submitting applications,
three offers came in at the same time. I was so happy.
Poor David was so proud of me once again. I felt so
blessed. I praised God for his timing and grace. I
remember praying to God for guidance and a clue as to
which was the best option because my Pro/Con list
routine wasn't working this time. I thanked Him for his
bounty and grace but puzzled about why He threw so
many options my way at once - knowing full well how
indecisive I could be and how multiple options in a big
decision paralyzed me.

Two of the three offers were interim positions.
One was full-time. That answered our main question. So,
I eagerly accepted the full-time option. I felt stressed but
fortunate to have had two weeks to get in there before
school started. I had no idea how large a mess I had
inherited. The place was filthy. I cleaned over an inch of
dust from under the circulation counter. Silverfish
scurried out of rips in the furniture. Books were not
organized according to district requirements and needed
to be shifted. I had help, but it wasn't enough. We

managed to get the place cleaned up and organized, but I still had no lesson plans ready for the first day of school – which was now a weekend away. Everyone kept telling me, "It's easy…Just try…Just do…" It was easy for them to say because they were experienced, former classroom teachers. I was completely new at this.

After staying up until 4:30 a.m. trying to pull lesson plans together, I resigned inside. I then decided to resign officially. I was unprepared both physically and professionally for the job. I was exhausted, frustrated and extremely sad. David and I had been so excited to get this job. It tore me up to give it up. Because of my failure, our finances once again grew tight as David's employer made some changes to their compensation structure. I felt awful and berated myself for being an utter failure. I chewed on it, analyzed every place I should of-could of-didn't do it right.

Fast forward a few months into 2013. I was offered another school librarian job. I thought for sure this was the one. The principal seemed so supportive and encouraging at first. So once again, I spent the entire summer cleaning out a media center only to resign shortly after school began due to an overwhelming situation. Yet another start-stop hiccup in my new career. I had burned yet another brand new bridge. I was embarrassed and ashamed. I berated myself daily for failing David and myself yet again. I exhausted myself with blow after blow of harsh self-talk and even a few very painful actual self-inflicted blows at myself. I hated me. I could not win. I wanted to hide. So I did.

God had other plans. He always does.

Finding Some Quiet

My dad was unable to speak when I saw him in the Hospice facility, but I could see recognition in his eyes. He smiled his sweet "dad" smile. After so many years of not being able to communicate with him, it was a true blessing to have gotten to see him and tell him how much I loved him. I thanked the Lord for this opportunity. It was so comforting to see my nephews, sisters and brothers-in-law surrounding my dad in his last days. We laughed. We sang. We talked with Dad and with each other. It felt good. It felt right.

Then we each took turns talking with him alone. When my turn came, my only words were to thank him for being my dad and for teaching me how to love. It was his greatest gift to this world. He and David were a lot alike in that regard. I had been my dad's sparring partner when it came to discussing politics or religion. Ironically, he played the devil's advocate in those debates. This time, all I could do was sit there silently, just holding my dad's hand and kissing his head, making sure I inhaled deeply so I could make memories of that familiar scent. The quiet felt right. It was comfortable – peaceful, in fact. I knew he would soon be going to a place where all would be revealed, and he would know what was on my heart. Words seemed unnecessary.

The next day Dad began to decline and slipped away after just a couple more days. That gentle man had been there to welcome me and my two sisters into the world. It was my honor to be there holding his hand as he breathed his last. As he lay there, I often closed my eyes and envisioned my sisters and I waiting with him, holding onto him and handing him over to Jesus. Heather read

Scripture, and we played his favorite hymns and sang "You Are My Sunshine" – his theme song. What peace and comfort we all found that day – in that moment at least.

Almost immediately after Dad left this earth, the poisons of this world bubbled over and out through some long simmering family hostilities. Things got noisy and even came close to blows. It was ridiculous. I just shook my head. Then I tried to intervene and convince them to think of Dad. "For Dad…Think of Dad," I tried to interject repeatedly. Nobody heard or cared. I quietly slipped out of the room and left them to their drama and noise. Lucky David had already escaped. He thought the family needed to be alone together. That makes me laugh out loud. Certain members of my family have no more business being alone together than a lit match and open gas line should be alone together.

It struck me as funny later because my dad had so frequently just wanted quiet. He often would say, "I just want some quiet." No wonder he enjoyed his job as a traveling salesman. He could actually get a few minutes of quiet. I could almost hear the little sarcastic guffaw he would utter when he made that request. He, too, tried to see the humor in at least some of this world's impossible situations.

No Escape

As always, David's response to the latest round of traumas and flying lead changes was quiet resignation and duty. He went to work. He took on more work. He went to bed. He went to work. He took on more work. He went to bed. He tried to help me feel better about things. Is it any wonder he started staying away? I felt so trapped and overwhelmed I wanted to be anywhere but where I was. How could I blame him for feeling that himself?

In an effort to find some quiet and escape his stress, David started spending hours after work hanging out in sports bars and restaurants alone. He stopped coming home right after work, and was spending countless hours away from home and me. When he came home, he never wanted to go out like we used to. I would wait at home, thinking we would be going out because we always had before. If we did go out to eat, he never wanted to eat. When I asked, he would say he was just tired or that he was trying to lose weight. He would just sit there, watching TV, drinking his beer, and counting the moments until he could go home to bed. He simply seemed to have withdrawn. This went on for several months. When we tracked it, we realized he also had spent thousands of our already limited dollars.

Things were just colliding on all sides. For the first time, I truly questioned David's love. I wondered why he had married me. It hurt to know that he preferred to be away from home for any length of time. I could not understand it. When I was stressed and hurting, home was the first place I turned. I failed to recognize that everyone handles difficult times differently. Once again, I took it out on myself by tearing myself down. I felt I had failed David. I felt pressure to fix the finances before they became a problem. I felt alone. I blamed myself. It was a vicious cycle that only God could break. And break it he did.

After several months of his new-found isolation, David broke down crying and confided to me that he thought he had a drinking problem. He picked the moment I was heading out the door to pick up one of our nephews to drop that bombshell. He also told me from the upstairs landing – nowhere near where I was standing. I hemmed and hawed between the door and hallway. I had to go. My nephew was waiting, but I couldn't go off and leave David like that. So, I dropped my purse and raced upstairs to at least hug David. I told him I didn't want to leave him like that, but he didn't want to ride with me so we could talk in the car. In true David fashion, he dried his tears and told me to go on. We could talk when I got back, he said.

I accompanied him to counseling which helped rectify at least the drinking and spending problem. However, trying to recoup the money we had lost to David's unexpected vice created more ongoing stress and anxiety for both of us. He committed to only an occasional beer and insisted he wanted to lose weight and even start running again. Little did we know how short-lived David's new-found focus on his health would be.

It was time to buck up and buckle down because God was not done with us yet. We were stuck in a time warp of side-tracks, back-tracks, start-stops and viciously jerking changes of direction: Good-bad-good-good-bad-good-bad-bad...uch. We were starting to get whiplash. We also forgot to duck.

Heavenly Father and Christ Jesus, my Lord, I pray...

Thank you for walking with me and showing your presence to me through the many losses I have suffered in this life. Thank you for holding on to me even when I lost my grip on you. Thank you for pulling me out of the depths of grief to give thanks to you and your grace and unfailing love. Thank you for the many people and creatures who have comforted me along the way. May I keep my eyes on you and honor you with unswerving trust. Thank you for my life.

In Jesus' name,
Amen

Chapter 6
Courage in the Battle

This is what the Lord says to you: "Do not be afraid or discouraged because of this vast army, For the battle is not yours, but God's.
...Stand firm and see the deliverance the Lord will give you...Do not be afraid; do not be discouraged. Go out and face them tomorrow, and the Lord will be with you."
- 2 Chronicles 20:15 and 17 (NIV)

Be strong and take heart, all of you who hope in the Lord.
- Psalm 31:24 (NIV)

"Do not be afraid, O man highly esteemed," he said.
"Peace! Be strong now; be strong."
- Daniel 10:19 (NIV)

Praise be to the God...of all comfort, who comforts us in all our troubles, so that we can comfort those in any trouble with the comfort we ourselves have received from God.
- 2 Corinthians 1: 3-4 (NIV)

David used to tell me he was proud of me for how I handled my treatment. He said he was proud of me for finishing my Library Science degree in the middle of chemo treatment. He was proud of me for having courage to change careers. If I were half as proud of me as David always said he was, I'd be a much more confident person.

I pray with sincerest hope that I made David feel as loved and proud of himself for the loving person and example of God's love he was as he always made me feel.

Friends have commented that I was perfectly equipped to help David through his battle because I had gotten through my own cancer treatment relatively unscathed. Yet what I have since realized is that David was the one who was best equipped to handle our trials. His gentle acceptance was like a quiet hand on me. I never gave him enough credit for that.

I was so proud of David for maintaining his level, gentle heart and quiet faith. It is what led him, even in the midst of all of our trials, to be looking out for someone else. One afternoon shortly after the completion of my treatments, David called me to let me know about a charge that would show up on our credit card. He explained that while he was getting gas he noticed a man who was having trouble paying for his gas. David said the Lord told him to help this stranger. So David paid for this stranger's gas. As the gas filled the tank, David filled the man with God's love. The man thanked David profusely and explained that his wife was going through cancer treatment and that in his haste and stress, he had forgotten his wallet and had no way to pay David. David simply put his hand on the man's shoulder, and said, "God's got this." The man thanked David and promised to pay it forward.

When I think back on that day, I wonder whose hand rested on David's shoulder when he felt overwhelmed. Whose hand comforted David when he heard difficult news?

A Quiet Courage

David always held tightly to the word of God. He knew it in his heart. He truly believed God "had this" and had already conquered this world. Yet I wonder, who counseled the counselor? Who in this world held him up? David could be hard to read. He never wanted anything. He never seemed to object. He rarely gave in to anger. He just lived his life in quiet acceptance and gentle obedience. What I did not realize until after he was gone was that his acceptance and obedience were not signs of indifference or weakness. In fact, I see now that it was a quiet courage. That courage would be tested to its limits in the next 14 months.

On December 1, 2014 sweet David woke up with severe abdominal pain which compelled us to head to the emergency room. What we thought was gallstones or some other gastrointestinal predicament ended up being inoperable Stage 4 metastatic pancreatic and liver cancer. The 8-centimeter mass was wrapped around some blood vessels. We knew without even asking what the prognosis was. Officially, he was given one year and a couple weeks to live. Boom. Just like that. Our train had officially derailed, and all the cars came barreling forward into a mangled mess. It did not stop there.

Another Diagnosis

Although we focused on each moment and just rolled with what unfolded, we both felt the weight of his diagnosis lurking over us. David started his journey in an emergency room which helped get him on the fast-track for CT scans and doctor's appointments. He spent days in a hospital being shuffled from scan to scan and procedure to procedure, test to test. They blocked the nerve around the tumor to alleviate some of the pain. They started him on pain meds and a blood thinner. Then they sent in the palliative care team.

The palliative care doctors filled us with enough information to fill a textbook series. They insisted that this was now about "quality of life." David and I both were surprised and offended by their immediate focus on the end of David's life. Why were we reading the last page first? It felt like they were writing David off. He said that very thing, in fact. They instantly went to the negative, the end…the loss. We knew what we were up against. We were seasoned war horses by now. This was not our first rodeo. We were not burying our head in the sand and ignoring the realities of the painful challenge with blind optimism or headstrong confidence, but nor were we ready to discuss pain management and giving up before we had even spoken with the oncologist to get the "official" prognosis. It was maddening.

I will never forget how suddenly small David looked physically. He appeared worn out and sad already. I could feel his fear and the sharp realization of his own mortality. I cried all the way home from the hospital when I had to leave him to go home to tend to the dogs. Leaving him in that dark place was agony. We could not get him out of there fast enough to suit me.

I continued to lose faith in David's initial medical care team when we met with his first oncologist – a very businesslike individual who could have benefited from a bedside manner refresher course. That doctor told us that David's prognosis was one year and a couple weeks. Then came information about the chemotherapy regimen options and the recommended course of treatment. Cut and dried. Done. That oncologist did reach out at one point to rub and hold on to David's knee – almost as if apologizing for delivering such news. After what that doctor put David through, it was the least she could do.

Getting Pushy

I find it interesting to compare how I handled David's diagnosis versus mine. Perhaps it was because I had been down this road before and knew what questions to ask and when. Perhaps it was just my protective side waking up and stepping in front of David. Perhaps it was because my diagnosis was "only" Stage 2 and my treatment had an end date whereas David's did not. Whatever the reason, I have concluded that it was easier to be the patient than the protector.

The battles feel longer and messier when you are fighting for someone else. I had to take care of everything. I found myself becoming an automaton and compartmentalizing my two worlds – the "normal" routine and the new normal of managing David's treatment and wrestling with the details (i.e., insurance coverage, coordinating David's leave time, finding health insurance when David's employer coverage terminated, talking with doctors and making sure David was comfortable and had everything he needed so he could focus on his fight, and finding a job). Every single phone call and issue was a battle. Nothing came easily. I have more battle scars from those 14 months of phone calls and details than I received from my own surgery and treatment.

During my own battle, I was more hopeful and accepting of each skirmish and potential outcomes. David's battle was more difficult to accept. It was blatantly unfair. Acceptance did not come as easily. I railed at God's plan now. I kept my shoulder in the yoke (or my face to the pavement, as it felt some days), but I was chafing now. The yoke felt like a massive millstone around my neck. All I could see was the struggle now. I could not fathom any good coming of it. I could not understand. I got angry. I beat myself up. I found myself asking *Why?* I found myself asking God to fix me for David's battle, to please fill the cracks so I would not shatter into bits. God answered. He always does. Unfortunately, He was asking me to just hang in there and trust. More skirmishes were on the horizon.

The Uphill Charge

David started a blistering series of chemo blasts called Folfirinox/5FU which ended up being too much for him. He carried a chemo pouch that cycled constantly and occasionally beeped. He had to keep the dogs at a distance to keep them from getting tangled in the tubing. Every hit made him violently ill, even creating temporary neurological issues and slurred speech. He stayed agitated, dehydrated and extremely ill and weak. He lost extreme amounts of weight in mere days. I seriously believe that David would not have lasted through even one more round of his initial oncologist's recommended treatment plan. Despite his reaction to his chemo regimen, his initial oncology group insisted that they wanted to, "Try it a couple more times and see what happens." Um…No, sir… I encouraged the doctor to take a look at

David, who was slumped over in a wheelchair, freezing and hurting – in utter agony. I informed them that if they touched David "a couple more times" they would be helping me plan David's funeral. I even reduced a Physician's Assistant to shaky tears. Talk about getting pushy! Enough was enough.

Before we got out of the parking lot that day, I was on the phone with my oncologist and the insurance company to switch David to my oncology team. Luckily it did not take long. We originally thought (because we were told) that David's treatment would only be considered in-network through his initial healthcare system because he had started treatment through their ER and because David's primary care physician was affiliated with it. I took a chance and looked into that. *Thank you, God.*

David's new treatment plan was a Gemcitabine combination – a much more easily tolerated regimen. Unfortunately, he started the new routine already weakened from his previous experience. The predicted and actual outcomes did not change David's prognosis. We did not really expect it to. At that point, it became about quality of life, not quantity. We refused to put a number on David's days, but we knew our time was limited. Rather than focusing on beating the cancer entirely and anticipating a miracle, we focused on living happily in spite of it. We tried anyway. Once again, the ground began eroding with every move. We lost traction with every step.

The Slippery Slope

One morning in January, I went in to tend to little old Sidney, our sweet, shy 20-year-old gray cat, but he had returned to Heaven at some point in the night. He was still curled up in his bed with his little face tucked down into the padding. Sweet little Sidney was pure sweetness. There was not a mean or mischievous bone in his tiny body. Sidney was David's other feline companion during his bachelor days and personal hardships. David somehow knew the source of my tears before I could even utter the words. Once again, this world had stripped away yet another warm comfort from us. Once again, I made the trek to the vet's office by myself, this time knowing that I was leaving David at home to suffer the initial loss alone. I cried all the way to the vet's office, sometimes reaching behind me to pat Sidney's soft gray fur – as if doing so would bring me any comfort. Without the gentle "peep" and purr, it only punched me harder.

Then just two months later, Tillman, our seven-year-old goofy love-bug of a Great Dane, was diagnosed with bone cancer. We began pain and anti-inflammatory medications. All I could do was cry – right there in the vet's office – completely alone in the dimly lit x-ray room. The vet kindly let me cry and collect myself before I went back into the room where sweet Tillman waited for my return, innocently wagging at me, not understanding why I was upset. I was now going to lose my big silly, one of my lights and greatest comforts in this world when I would need him most.

I ended up caring for two cancer patients simultaneously. Both of them had mobility issues, both were declining, and Tillman weighed more than me even at the end. We eventually decided to amputate Tillman's back leg to alleviate his pain, but it was too late. We were still going to lose him. We knew it. I was (and will always be) heartbroken.

Interference

As if David were not suffering enough with his physical battle, the dark one began stirring up emotional and family interference. Around the Christmas of 2014, at the urging of David's close family member, one of David's ex-girlfriends started texting and trying to reconnect with David. She certainly meant no harm, but poor David was so out of it, he did not even remember when it started. The constant texting and interference agitated David so greatly that he would be violently sick to his stomach and so confused he could not remember his own phone number.

When David tried to stop the communication, David's family member lashed out at me – even blaming me for David's cancer and decline. David was instantly angry and confused about why this was happening. He could not fathom how someone who claimed to love him could do such a thing. Long story short, we ended up getting a restraining order against David's close family member on top of everything else. Imagine poor David, in his weak and painful state and barely able to stand, having to stand before a judge to take such action. It was bitterly painful to witness.

Once again, I blamed myself for David's additional hardship. Surely I could have prevented this, I thought. What I failed to remind myself was that, as painful as it was, it is what David wanted – and even needed. As always, he was trying to protect me – just as I was trying to protect him. But who had his hand on David at that moment? I wondered.

A Glimmer

For months after David's diagnosis, I tried unsuccessfully to secure a full-time position in either corporate communications or education. I submitted hundreds of applications to no avail. My well had dried up. Once again, I berated and pummeled myself. As I submitted one application for a school librarian job, I said, "That's it. If this one does not work, I'm done." I prayed to God that if this was the opportunity he wanted for me, then he needed to make it so. He answered. He did.

I started a new job as the school librarian at the best school in the universe – Lewisville Elementary School. I spent the entire summer cleaning out yet another media center, but it was so worth it. It is a sweet, cozy little media center. David got to visit once during the summer – wearing pajama bottoms, a tee shirt and a jacket. By then he was walking with a cane.

He was so proud of me, and he said in his now wispy voice, "I feel you here. I see you here." I caught him leaving a sticky note in my top desk drawer. Tears stung my eyes when I saw his equally wispy handwriting. The note read, *"I love you! You do make a difference. – D"* Just as when David proposed to me, I hugged David and held on tight. I looked at that note every morning before work – even after David's return to Heaven. Even then, he was still looking out for me and comforting me.

The only challenge was the location – 34 miles one way. I missed so many days to care for David that I would have to repeat my first year. The gracious principal and staff never complained. They tried in every way to accommodate me and ease my burden. The challenge was too much for me in that time. They knew it but held onto me anyway. Yet I knew even repeating my first year was not the worst thing that would happen to me in the coming year.

The top rail clattered to the ground.

Heavenly Father and Christ Jesus, my Lord, I pray...

Thank you for helping me find the courage and strength to protect David through his suffering. Thank you for granting me the discernment to know when it was right to stand up for myself and David. Thank you equally (perhaps more) for the discernment to know when to stand down and trust that your will would be done despite attempts to tear us down. Thank you for being my shield and my fortress. May I show your protection and love to others.

In Jesus' name,
Amen

Chapter 7
Waiting for Jesus

Wait for the Lord; be strong and take heart and wait for the Lord.
- Psalm 27:14 (NIV)

"...Wait for the gift my Father promised, which you have heard me speak about."
- Acts 1:4 (NIV)

I waited patiently for the Lord; he turned to me and heard and my cry.
- Psalm 40:1 (NIV)

They tell how you turned to God...and to wait for his Son from heaven, whom he raised from the dead – Jesus, who rescues us from the coming wrath.
- 1 Thessalonians: 10 (NIV)

    David was a wispy shadow of his former physical self at the start of 2016. He was down to less than 95 pounds (if that). He was skin and bone. He was feeble. He slept 24/7, often with open, unseeing eyes and long pauses between breaths. He could barely stand on his own anymore. He had been in and out of the hospital to receive intravenous fluids and to relieve frequent shortness of breath. He had battled the discomfort of ascites and losing his taste for everything but spaghetti with marinara sauce. He wore a DNR bracelet instead of a watch. His abdominal catheter required draining daily. Of course, by this point, he was not producing as much fluid as he had been. He held out as long as he could, but we eventually had to bring in a Hospice team and equipment.

David's spiritual self was still there though. In fact, his faith was stronger than it had ever been. He quietly accepted that he was nearing the end of this life. He had accepted it. He just wanted the suffering to stop. His lingering question was why the Lord did not just come for him. Why did the suffering have to continue for so long? How was it good for anyone? He was struggling to understand. We all were. We were facing the tallest fence of all. Yet we moved forward. Stopping in our tracks was still not an option.

Clearing tall hurdles requires many factors to be working together – speed, strength, distance. Sometimes you have to back up a bit to build up your momentum. That's what God was asking us to do - again.

The Cliff

On February 9 (the day before David's last birthday) I caught my first glimpse of the impending cliff. Almost one year after being diagnosed with bone cancer, my beloved Big Silly, Tillman, returned to Heaven. A couple months before, we had opted to have his rear left leg amputated because his leg and foot were swelling so badly. Once again, it became about quality of life, not quantity. Now Tillman's breathing had changed. Our phenomenal veterinarian had made multiple house calls and special trips to help me load Tillman in the car because I could not manage that by myself. On this trip, he managed to get us in to use a local vet's facilities so we would not have to drive as far. While there, Tillman started coughing up blood. I knew without seeing the x-rays that the cancer had spread, and that we were done. Dr. Humphrey rode back to the house with me so Tillman could take his leave at home. My sweet bubba silly rested on his big bed with his head in my lap – a well-practiced, quite natural pose. We had spent countless hours like that so many times before. I petted him softly and nestled my face near his soft ear. He always smelled like warm buttered popcorn. As Dr. Humphrey administered the dose, I whispered, "I love you, Bubba. It's okay. Run on ahead. We'll be along. See you there." I felt Tillman grow cold, and I just collapsed into tears. Poor David could barely stand up himself, but he struggled up to comfort me. That was the first time I felt a new kind of alone. It would not be the last.

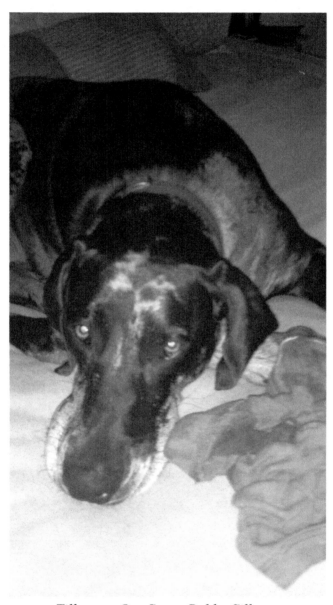

Tillman – Our Sweet Bubba Silly

The Rest Stop

Just a few weeks after Tillman's return to Heaven, David began to decline rapidly. David was confined to a hospital bed. He sipped grape Kool-Aid and took nips of chocolate pudding. He was taking morphine and other strong pain medications. Swallowing became a challenge so even the tiniest of pills had to be crushed and soaked in water. A syringe was the only way to administer them. We knew without words that our time was getting small. Once again, words seemed unnecessary. The most often repeated words were, "I love you." Always David would open his eyes weakly and whisper back, "I love you, too." When his sister, her husband and their daughter left to return home he roused himself enough to tell them to "drive safe." As always he was looking out for others. As always he was the comforter.

Ordering Pizza

By this time, David was too weak to walk to the bathroom and had started to use a bedside commode. One evening when I was holding him up and helping him get dressed and back in bed, he said he wanted to go out. Of course, he was in no condition to go anywhere, but I played along. I asked him where we should go. He inquired sweetly in his wispy voice with a tickle of a smile, "How about pizza?" I smiled because pizza had always been one of his favorites. I guided him back into bed and assured him I thought that was a great idea.

As I settled him back in bed and fixed the sheets around him and adjusted his pillows, he indicated that the line for the pizza place was long. "They're busy here," he pointed out. I told him to sit down and that I'd go to the counter to order. I asked him what he wanted on his pizza. He recited his usual toppings of choice – pepperoni, green peppers and onions. I teased him then by adding, "...and black olives?" David hated black olives. He whispered firmly with a down tilt of his head, "No black olives." I asked him again just for fun. Even in his weak state, he answered in the same firm whisper and tilt, "No black olives." I chuckled then, and he smiled wanly. He was on to me.

We sat there in companionable silence for a few minutes, just holding hands – like we used to do when we were dating. Once again he commented on how busy the place was. Then David said, "They're sure taking a long time." I told him I would check on it and that it was probably taking so long because they were so busy. I waited a minute then informed him that they were working on it.

While we "waited," David whispered sweetly, "Do you think Jesus likes pizza?" I assured him that Jesus would eat pizza if it would make us happy (even the pepperoni).

"Do you think Jesus would eat pizza with us?" he inquired quietly. Again, I assured him that Jesus would be happy to eat with us. "He's sure taking a long time," David said wistfully. "He's late." In a broken voice, I assured my sweet man that Jesus was on his way. I felt a sudden, warm peace in the truth of my words.

Best Friends

David was starting to leave us. I was starting to come unglued. I could not manage his physical needs. David would get stiff and start hurting. He had an ongoing raw spot on his tailbone. He had to be moved periodically to prevent stiffness and more sores. The pauses between his breaths were getting longer and longer. He had lost feeling in one of his legs. Before getting a catheter, he needed help getting to the bedside commode. It was 24/7 monitoring and care. A Hospice nurse was coming daily. David's parents were a huge help. As a retired nurse, David's mom knew different ways to help move him and administer medications. *Thank you, God.*

Even with the support we had, I felt so helpless and tired, I was growing angry. Once when David asked if I would go get his mom to help him move, I lost it. I felt as if someone had attached me to a boulder and dropped me straight down. I was so hurt. I lost my patience even with his ever-patient parents. Unfortunately, they left the next day. I am sad I hurt their feelings. David's mom was completely understanding and forgiving, despite her own pain over the incident. She said it was like when a best friend moves away. The other friend gets mad to make it easier to say goodbye. That was the perfect analogy. My best friend was leaving me.

The Veil

On March 21, 2016, sweet, gentle David flew to his beloved Jesus and returned to Heaven. He slipped away quietly and with a big, sudden smile on his face. It was wonderful to see. All day he had held a simple wooden cross in his hand. He was still holding on to it. It is an honor to have witnessed a gentle, happy passing for such a gentle spirit as his.

During his last days, David was surrounded by loving family and friends. Over the last week or so, he and I had many nice quiet moments together that I will treasure always. As he moved in and out of consciousness or sleep, he frequently looked for Jesus. He also talked a lot about going home. He would ask, "Are we home yet?" and "When are we going home?" and "Let's go home…I want to go home." He even saw through the veil a few times, often asking, "Who are all those people with you?" "Who's that with you?" When I asked him if they were smiling and friendly, he always said they were. He said they were nice. One time he even said they were waving. What comforting images!

He once saw a guy in red "with no expression" (I'm still puzzling about that one.) Other times he asked, "Are you coming with me?" He even asked in his now whispery, feeble voice if he could hit me over the head so I could go with him. I told him I would if I could. Then I just held his hand, rested my head in his neck, and hugged him tightly.

On a fun note…David was looking out for me even after he left. Our landscape lights had been off for months after a power outage a few months earlier. Our front porch light fixture was occupied by an adorable bird's nest, so we were unable to turn it on. Several months prior to that, despite his feeble condition, David was trying to be helpful and change a light bulb, but the neuropathy in his hands caused him to drop the glass surround from the fixture. It shattered to bits. As the funeral service representatives carried David's body down the steps on a gurney, I noticed that the landscape lights had come back on. Love that! Once again, David was looking out for others.

David won! He made it home! Praise God! David's suffering was over. *Thank you, God.*

Heavenly Father and Christ Jesus, my Lord, I pray...

Thank you for welcoming David home with open arms and the comfort and warmth of your love. He suffered so much physically in his time here. Thank you for giving him the rest and peace he so long sought. Thank you for blessing my life with a man such as David. Because of him, because of his wonderful example, I will walk more closely with you. He was truly one of your finest angels. I will miss him every day, but I find comfort in your promise that we will be reunited in love with you and live forever in your ever-loving presence.

In Jesus' name,
Amen

Chapter 8
Triumph and Tribute

But thanks be to God, who always leads us in triumphal procession in Christ and through us spreads everywhere the fragrance of the knowledge of him.
- 2 Corinthians: 2:14 (NIV)

Jesus said to her, "I am the resurrection and the life. He who believes in me will live, even though he dies; and whoever lives and believes in me will never die. Do you believe this?"
- John 11:25 (NIV)

"His master replied, 'Well done, good and faithful servant! You have been faithful with a few things; I will put you in charge of many things. Come and share your master's happiness!'"
- Matthew 25:21 (NIV)

David knew he would not die even when his body did. He held tight to his plain wooden cross – a special gift he received at the beginning of his journey. He simply waited – patiently, longingly. He was ready to go home. Many times in his last hours he would mutter, "I love Jesus!" I would reassure him that Jesus loved him, too. He would whisper, "I hope I did all right." The sweetness of that statement always brought tears to my eyes. Who else could live better than David had? I reassured him that he had been a good and faithful servant, and that he had made God and Jesus proud. David would just nod or flash a tiny smile. I could see in his eyes that he was comforted by that knowledge.

As I thought about David's Celebration of Life service, it occurred to me that love truly is the greatest of all. Our faith may wobble at times. Our hope may fade occasionally. Yet love (once we experience it and offer it) remains constant – and grows stronger. It has the power to hold us up when all else fails.

David's whole life was a testament to love. Everything he did was to help someone else. He sought – and seized – every opportunity to demonstrate not just love, but Christ's love, to every creation on earth. That is why it was so important to me that David knew how very much he was loved.

Throughout David's treatment, I would ask him multiple times a day at random moments and always before going to sleep, "Do you know how loved you are?" He told me he did, but as his treatment took its toll on his body, I worried what it might be doing to his heart and his spirit. Sadly, he is unable to answer me now, but I think he knows how loved he was – and not just by me. Shortly after his diagnosis, my brother-in-law, Jim, and I compiled a bunch of pictures of David and the many people who loved him and set it to a sweet love song that meant a great deal to us. David was so touched he cried. He didn't know what to say.

Since his journey began in December 2014, David had lost over 130 pounds – a shadow of his former self. Once, while in the hospital emergency room, David walked by two little boys, one of whom stared at David's emaciated face and inquired softly, *"Oooo! What kind of man is this?"* Again, God spoke through the most unexpected angels.

Their innocent words were not meant to be harmful, but David suddenly felt self-conscious and worried that his appearance was scaring little kids. However, their words made me think…Why not ask those who know David to answer that question? Why not tell David what kind of man we think he is? Their responses confirmed that David is much more that his physical appearance. Those who did not know David responded with their prayers for sweet David. I read each one aloud to him. He knew without question how loved he was!

Tribute

David is a rare sort of man. I often thank him for asking me to marry him and be his life partner. David is the kindest and best of men. He is a man of few words, but his feelings and sensitivity run deeper than the world could ever see. His first instinct is to help others – always. No matter what he is going through, he seeks to help others first. Even in the midst of his own cancer treatment, he put himself aside and sought to help others find a relationship with Christ. He wanted so badly to know that he made a difference to others and that he helped others. It has been my privilege and honor to know and love David. He has held me up and encouraged me. I could not ask for a better husband. He is a rare and special treasure – from God himself indeed.

- PJ Frick

_____

We are truly blessed to have David as our son. He has always been kind and thoughtful. He has always been there supporting us when we needed help and when we didn't. He has been a friend and co-Clemson Fan, sharing trips to games.

He tends to put other's needs ahead of his own. He has brought us a wonderful daughter-in-law in PJ. He is deeply loved and loving.

We always remember the day he came home from kindergarten all excited because he was born on "Ham Lincoln's" birthday.

He has been a hard worker, and has helped others to achieve their goals.

That is the kind of man David is, and we love him.

Mom and Dad [iii]

David has been like a brother to me. We were inseparable from 1971-1984. Then college and jobs/life separated us physically but not spiritually. We've always stayed in touch.

I owe David for all his encouraging words throughout our friendship; especially during my time at the Academy. I'm not sure I would have made it through that place without him motivating me.

He's always been there for me. He stayed my friend when I was held back (flunked) 1st grade. It would've been easy to move on without me. He was at my Academy graduation. He was there when I proposed to Toni. He was and still is my Best Man! He and you have been very generous and kind remembering Nicholas' b'day!

I think in a word...David is Faithful. I'm grateful to have him as a friend and very lucky to count him as a brother!! I love y'all! Hope this helps.

Love, Johnny[iv]

You have been in my thoughts so often. I was thinking back to the first time we met. It was a couple years ago, I believe, I met you and PJ as you were coming into Waxhaw United Methodist Church as visitors. For the next several months, I looked forward to seeing you two for our short, "Hello, and good to see you!" Before long, your kind gentle smile made me feel we could be on hugging terms – so hugs became our new greeting. I always love having new friends to hug! So thank you for that kind smile and a new friendship with you and sweet PJ.

Please know that you and PJ are in my thoughts and prayers.

Love to you.
Susan Johnson[v]

For me, David is a best friend and my wnc barbecue and wing buddy (when we could both eat it). He's been a pillar of support through all the rough times and the same pillar through all of the good. A friend who is always a phone call away and will ask about your day even when his isn't going so well.

Really, I've seen David as a rock. He's a support, we both have talked about how hard it is to accept help from others when we are always there to help those others. But we have both given and accepted help from each other with relative ease.

My best times with David have always been over a plate of good bbq just being able to complain and spout off about things and in the next sentences talk about all of the good things as well.

So. To those kids I'd say (not to freak them out)...he's a man, he's a man who has given to others, cared for others and accepted care from others. A man who laughs like anyone else and cries that way too. A man whose will is strong and has been fighting to be able keep giving, spending of himself to be who he is.

Scott Spencer[vi]

David is a kind, caring, considerate, thoughtful man who is always willing to help "all creatures great and small." I remember when you and David invited us to cookout at your house years ago. David made us feel immediately at home. He's a tough soldier to go through what he has been through and has a good heart and strong faith.

Love,
Susan & Al
Keeping you & David in our prayers[vii]

How beautiful PJ.

You are awesome! And so is David! As you know you and I went through a traumatic time in our lives – together. What I remember, and what will always sick with me, is David reaching out to me because of your situation. He was so concerned about you and your journey – he wanted to help YOU and be supportive in any way possible. He is a great husband with a strong faith and I so admire that about him – so concerned about you and your options and your lives together. He wanted to learn what he could to help you in your very personal fight. So, because of him initiating the conversation with me about cancer treatment options he got you more information on possible ways to navigate your course.

His initiative helped you in your journey. So, I am grateful for David for having the courage to ask me questions – it shows his commitment to you and your lives together. It doesn't get much better than that! I emphasize this because I have a friend who went through thyroid cancer. Now, 3 years later, her marriage is on the rocks, she is wondering why and how things in their relationship got so bad? He drops a bombshell: He told her he pulled away from her and withdrew after her diagnosis because he thought she was going to die. How absolutely awful!! She had to not only go the course alone but with her husband in the background not communicating his fears with her so they could work on that together. Luckily they are trying to come to terms with that now but this story is just a testament to you two and your love and care for one another.

We are all going to die – nobody gets out alive but what you do while you're here, the way you 'live' your commitments to one another makes happiness possible in each moment. I would rather have that than being alive yet living separately with a partner who fears for what tomorrow may hold – nobody is promised that. Now is all you have. And my prayer and thought for you and David: "Joy gives us wings." Your love for one another is palpable. Keep on keepin' on! Lastly, you know I am a dog person and I know also what a good dog Daddy David is and how much your animals bring such daily joy into your home and your lives.

Much love,
Becky[viii]

Thanks for the update! Please know that the Lord continually brings David to my mind, and I pray for him often, and that is a sincere and honest statement, and not just something nice to say!!

First of all, as one who has worked with David during his career..., I can truly say that he has made an impact on many people's lives, and he is sincerely missed by me and his co-workers.

I inherited several of David's Vocational Rehabilitation files, and when I shared with the injured workers and attorneys why David was no longer working with his clients, the response was visible shock and disappointment, with hope that David would return to work soon. Several of his clients... and others (including attorneys and adjusters) had nothing but positive things to say about the kind of person that David IS, and that they would be praying for him!!! A couple of them even shed tears for David, since they really cared about him. Which is rare, given the nature of the business that we are in... lol!!

David has definitely left his mark and a positive impression on **ALL** who know him, and although we did not work closely together (due to the nature of our business) I always appreciated knowing that David was a fellow brother in the Lord, and considered him a professional partner in this business. David has a positive spirit about him, and a humbleness that is clearly visible, and I believe it is his faith in the Lord that is shining through for others to see and feel, in his own quiet way.

I pray for David (and you) a lot, and continually ask the Lord to give him a healing touch, comfort, let him feel His presence and feel the love of the friends and family that are around him. Please tell David that although we may not talk, he has and will continue to be in my thoughts and prayers!!

Blessings to both of you,
Lee Anzaldi
Co-worker and brother in the Lord[ix]

What kind of man is David Frick? I'll share some and maybe you can pass it along to those two boys.

When I think of David, the first thing that comes to mind is being a fighter. Without firsthand experience, I can't imagine what the last 14 months have been like for David. I guess no one knows how they will do in such a situation until it is upon them, but I have admired his courage and determination as we have talked together this past year.

And I know he has fought this fight well, because he has continued to focus on others instead of himself. He has asked how he could help others, asked about others in the church who are going thorough times of suffering, and he has always thought of you, PJ, and how you are struggling through it all. Doubts, fears, and discouragement are all expected when fighting a terrible disease, but he has not given in to bitterness, anger or self-pity. It is humbling for me to watch.

David is a man of integrity. I see this most in his honesty. David is not one to dominate a conversation, but from those early small groups at our house, he has always been forthright and authentic in his sharing. As a pastor, I see all sorts of people who try to put up fronts and masks to hide their true selves, but I never had the slightest hint of that from David. For me, that is a great sign of integrity. None of us have it all together, and being able to acknowledge that and be able to share that truth with others is a great step toward wholeness and having an integrated life.

I have been glad to share his journey of faith. From hearing his stories of Catholic school (and the clicker) to where God has brought him today, I see God at work in his life. Not only does he trust in God, but he desires that others grow in their relationship with God as well.

David is a caring and loving man and I know you know this most of all, PJ.

I thank you for this email. I hope many people will be able to express their love for you and David in this way.

Keep me posted.

May the Love of God hold you close,
John[x]

This is what I think of David:
Doing God's work by helping others survive in today's job
 environment
Always thinking of ways to help others
Vowing to never give up
Intellectually thinking outside of the box
Doing the right thing
Forgiving people when they are at their worst
Rising above all to make someone feel comfortable
Inspirational to others
Culturally Sensitive
Keeping the faith, he has a plan for everyone.
"People will forget what you said. People will forget what
 you did, but people will never forget how you made them
 feel."...Maya Angelou
- Janet Gordon[xi]

When Pastor John first came, he asked for a night of
prayer at the church. I remember giving an emotional
testimony about my heart break and crying. This was
before he knew of his own cancer. I remember the both
of you, (you both had no connection with me yet at all),
came up to me and told me you'd pray for me. I
remember him being very direct in his engagement with
me that he'd pray and seemed very committed to that
statement.

It was shortly after that he found out about his own
struggle. I've tried to show the kind of commitment in
prayer that he showed me that night. My struggles turned
out to be minor compared to what sweet man has had to

endure. That memory during that night of prayer at WUMC has been an inspiration for me. David showed me God's love that night. I still remember it to this day.

Sent with love and gratitude to my church family member, Mr. David Frick,

Pat Dussinger[xii]

I didn't get to know David personally but what I do know OF him, he is wonderful husband and caring person. I remember passing by the library a few days this summer and saw him helping you set up. He was so excited because YOU were so excited. I also remember you telling me that even on days when he was very sick, he encouraged you to go work. He knows how you love your job (but I know you love him more). I also remember that on our first chilly fall morning, he was concerned about children whom may not have coats. Even while facing his own terrible battle, he was thinking of others. That says a lot about a person.

I hope this helps.

Kim Morton[xiii]

My Dear PJ,

As you and David both know, I have never met David. However, knowing you and listening to you and knowing what I do of the path you two have been on and the love you have for each other (and your fur babies!), I ask you to tell David from me that I know what a good person he is. Strong. Steadfast. A good and faithful heart. And a man who loves his wife. A man strong in faith.

It is my firm belief that David has impacted more people than he will ever know. People watch and observe. And our actions truly are the best indicators of who we really are.

Please pass this along. And my love for you both.

Kisses,
Bonnie[xiv]

Hi, PJ!
You've been on my mind a lot lately....as has David. Continuing to pray for you both.

I have never met David, but I feel like I know him in some ways through my friendship with you. I've always felt that he is the kind of man to put others' needs first and to go the extra mile to help others or ensure they get the help they need. I felt like his job was evidence of that kind of character and strength. In my prayers for David in this difficult and challenging time, I have asked God to give him the peace, wisdom and strength that he need to minister to and to continue to help others. I believe he has made a difference in the lives of people he has already touched and I believe he has the ability to touch more lives with his unique gifts and strengths.

Like I said, PJ....I am continuing to pray. You're special to me...hope you know that!
Love,
Kathy[xv]

Hello Dear PJ,

Of course, I don't know David well and have only met you maybe two or three times in my life, but I know in my heart how good you two are. I perceive your David as someone so very brave and amazing, given all he is going through. He is such a wonderful example of one who knows he is truly in the hands of his Maker and having complete trust in Him going forward. What wonderful examples both of you are for all of us.

Know you are loved and prayed for each and every day.
Aunt Annie xo[xvi]

Well, PJ, I don't know David; I know You and have met Your Mother.

What I thought of David, when John and I first met the two of you at church, I was impressed with the way that David looked at you with such a look of Love and Tenderness. His manners towards you were so Caring, that you were not just his wife; you are the Most Precious Human Being on earth.

Carmen Davidson[xvii]

Angel of God my guardian dear, to whom God's love entrust David my dear; ever this day be at his side, to light and guard, to rule and guide; Amen!

Uncle Nick Moorman[xviii]

PJ.

Good to hear from u and my apologies for not doing a better job of keeping in touch. With two sets of grandkids most of our communicating goes in that direction.

Hope things are going as good as could be expected. It has to be a hard thing living with your realities day after day. Yes, you are in my prayers. While that process is pretty fluid, most of the time it goes something like this:

Lord. You have given us the gift of David with everything he brings to those around him. I ask your blessing on him. Let him know you are with him in the good times and the bad times. In the midst of everything, Lord, give him the gift of your peace.

It's not as formal as that but the thoughts are the same! I'll give you a call sometime soon (yes I truly will!!) and we can talk in greater detail.

Uncle Ronnie[xix]

I think it is a wonderful idea about what you are asking friends to do!

I got to know David thru PJ. We have spent times eating out and in our homes which are good times, good food and good conversations. David and Mike enjoy talking about their favorite past times- guns and movies and TV shows. David is a caring and compassionate man. I saw that in him even before I got to meet him as he was always at the stop to pick PJ up after work - I don't know of many guys that would do this for their wives. He is also passionate about his love for animals be it his cat or dogs - even rescuing one from a parking lot! I am sure he showed the same care and compassion for his clients in his job. He was a great help mate for PJ as she went thru her own battle with cancer.

We pray that David will be encouraged by your project PJ! Praying for both of you as you continue on this journey.

Keep up posted if there is anything we can do for you two.

Sending hugs to you both!

Love, Phyllis^{xx}

David is a very caring person and puts others before himself on so many occasions. He also cares for animals and has taken in rescue animals so many times.

I remember when we were little and would get sent to our rooms, we'd sit by the vent in our rooms and talk to each other. We could hear each other through the vents.

I had a blue metal peddle car and he had an orange peddle tractor that we rode on in our driveway.

When we were a little older, in elementary school, David didn't like his hair very short and lots of people thought he was a girl until they got to know him of course.

We used to arm wrestle and I would beat him because I was still bigger than him and had longer arms. That only lasted until he caught up with me though.

There was an empty lot beside the house we lived in before the house mom and dad have now. We played in the woods with friends lots. There was one tree right at the edge of the yard by the woods that had a limb that grew parallel to the ground and then turned perpendicular to itself and went straight up. We would get on that limb and hang upside down. David liked climbing trees and his friend too.

We both had banana seat bikes and would ride up and down the street with our friends. One end of the street was a hill and a piece of property that had a steep hill going up into the property. There wasn't a house there at that time. We would ride our bikes up and down that orange dirt hill into that property.

One time we went fishing as a family and I went to cast out my line and David was right behind me and the hook got caught near his eyebrow I think it was. Another time I jerked a fish out and it slung back and hid Dad in the face. I was a dangerous little fishergirl, lol.

I remember he and I playing with some plastic cowboy and indian figurines. We each picked either indians or cowboys and we'd each line them up in front of us and throw something, don't remember what, at each other's figures. The one that got all the other's down first won.

David played sports: basketball, baseball, and wrestling.

I have lots of memories.

I remember when he was 2 and had the croup and went in the hospital and I had to stay with our grandma Frick.

I have a couple of pictures of him sitting sideways in chairs in the den with his legs going over one arm and leaning back on the cushion in the chair. I guess it was more comfortable for him at that time. I'd say he was 11 maybe.

We played in the creek behind mom and dad's current home and caught craw dads.

We would go sailing as a family at Lake Murray and David and I would jump over board and swim. I remember he held me under water one time, which I didn't like because I wasn't that confident in the water. He loved the water. He jumped off the high dive at the Murraywood pool and liked surfing. I only heard about the surfing since I was probably at Clemson then.

David played his drums upstairs in the room over the garage, which was a pretty good place to play them.

I remember when David was little, he didn't have much interest in school and didn't do as well as most would like, but when he was a freshman in high school, he made all A's and as you know went on to Clemson and got his masters.

David came to visit us in IN when Kristen was 9 months old and he got to see her take her first step. He was excited about that.

This has turned into a fairly long email. Will let you know if I think of anything else.

Love,
Janet Lord[xxi]

Dear David,

I've been thinking about you for the past couple of weeks. I guess it's been over a year since you have been diagnosed with cancer. I bet you remember the day and time exactly. I can't imagine what you have gone through this year, and I can't imagine what is still ahead in your journey.

I have been thinking and praying for you and wanted to share some thoughts. I think it is remarkable that you have been fighting for your life this year when all the medical odds were against you. In so many ways, you are my hero, David, for continuing to fight. I think God has used you this past year to show perseverance and determination. As you have clung to your faith in Christ, I know that many people have grown closer in their relationship to God. Thank you for your verbal affirmation of your faith time and time again.

Now I think God is going to use you in a different way as you look to Hospice and the decisions that lie there. God is the creator of life, and I am so thankful that God has allowed me to know both of you. You have blessed me more than you will ever know. God is also the one who calls us back to him, and I think the faithful witness in death is as powerful as the faithful witness in life. I know it can't be easy, and my prayers continue to be with you.

You have fought a good fight, David! Now I pray for peace as you prepare for what is next and cling to Jesus, the author and prefector of our faith.

I love you and PJ,

Anita

The Lord your God is with you.
He is mighty to save.
He takes great delight in you.
He quiets you with his love,
And rejoices over you with singing.
Zeph. 3:17 [xxii]

My brother-in-law, David Frick, used to come over to watch whatever game was on that day. We once watched the first college football game of the season – between two teams I'd never heard of before – just because it was football. And then there were the times he'd suggest a movie I never thought I'd want to see – say, *Dumb and Dumber* or *Wild Hogs* – and I'd buy it from iTunes and stream onto the big screen at my house. And we'd grab a beer and laugh hysterically. And before the game or the movie was over, David would tell me what we should watch next time.

And there was always a next time.

And David was a huge Clemson fan. Yet, it never seemed to bother him that I am a Tarheel. He never mentioned it when Clemson would make a mockery of Carolina on the football field, yet he never failed to mention when Carolina basketball dominated his beloved Tigers on the hardwood. One year, we bought a pizza and made wings and watched the Carolina-Clemson basketball game at my house. Clemson led 39 of the 40 minutes of the game, and someone made a last-second floater in the lane to put the Heels on top just as the clock expired. I felt awful. I really did. I told David that I just knew Clemson would win next time.

And there would always be a next time.

About 15 months ago, David went to the Emergency Room for what might have been an appendicitis or a problem with his gall bladder. Only it wasn't. It was pancreatic cancer. Stupid. Horrible. Merciless. Pancreatic Cancer.

And all of a sudden, there were fewer next times.

David fought valiantly against the Cancer and the Chemo and the onslaught of complications. But he didn't make it over for as many big games after that visit to the ER.

I would have given anything to have had him over for the ACC Football Championship between Clemson and Carolina a few months ago. Don't tell any of my Carolina friends, but I was happy to see the Tigers take it. For

David. And I so wanted Clemson to roll over the Crimson Tide!

Maybe next time.

On my birthday, David texted me, "If I was not so ill, I would bring you a giant beer." And maybe a simple text doesn't sound like such a big deal, but it just goes to show who David was. He was fighting for his life and yet, he still had time to send birthday wishes and share a smile.

Over the last couple of weeks, David has been mostly confined to a hospital bed that Hospice brought in and set up in the den of their home. When we have visited, my mind has struggled to reconcile the frail shell of a man before me with everything I knew to be inside the soul and being of David Frick. Everything he has meant to me. To everyone. The difference he has made in this world. I was in the room with David, but I couldn't truly connect.

For whatever reason, I decided to grab a six-pack on the way over to visit David last night. "Cheers!" I said as I sat down on the couch next to the hospital bed. And how I wished David could have joined me in that toast. How I wished we could have laughed at some mindless comedy. Or loudly cheered on the Clemson Tigers. But despite what we weren't able to share, I was reminded of all the fun we had shared over the years. And I enjoyed the time and the beer and the memories while David rested quietly. And I felt a certain peace in that moment. And I think maybe my heart knew that this would be the last beer I'd enjoy with my brother-in-law.

So, Cheers to you, David! I know you are looking down from above with a glass raised.

Until next time.
Jim Denny[xxiii]

The Greatest of These

David and I both always connected to the verse in 1 Corinthians 13. We even had the Scripture numbers engraved on the inside of our wedding bands (1 Cor 13). It is a Scripture passage commonly used at weddings, but it somehow seemed just right for David's Celebration of Life service. When I first mentioned it to our pastor, I wanted to make sure he understood how it was so appropriate for David's service. I told him it was significant because I could substitute the word "love" in that passage with "David." To me, that showed how David met all of our Lord's criteria for living a life of love and service to others. How many of us can say that?

Our pastor did a wonderful job of holding David up as an example of love in this world and showing that David truly lived a life of love – specifically, Christ's love. People even commented after the service how humbled they were by it and how it showed them the areas they needed to work on in their own lives. *Thank you, God. Thank you, David.*

Love... *David...*
is patient, *is patient,*
Love is kind. *is kind.*

It does not envy,
It does not boast,
It is not proud.
It is not rude,
It is not self-seeking,
It is not easily angered,
It keeps no record of wrongs.
Love does not delight in evil
but rejoices with the truth.
It always protects,
always trusts, always hopes,
always perseveres.
Love never fails...
And now these three remain:
Faith, hope and love.
But the greatest of these is
love.

does not envy,
does not boast,
is not proud.
is not rude,
is not self-seeking,
is not easily angered,
keeps no record of wrongs.
does not delight in evil but
rejoices with the truth.
always protects,
always trusts, always hopes,
always perseveres.
never fails...

- 1 Corinthians 13:4-8, 13

Heavenly Father and Christ Jesus, my Lord, I pray:

Thank you for being a God of love. Please make me better than I was yesterday. Fill me with your peace and grace so that I may fill others with the same peace and grace you show to me always. May the world see you through me. Show me how to live a life of love and service so that I, too, may be an example for others in this world. Guide my tongue, my actions, and my heart so that I may honor you. Through you, with you, we cannot fail. Thank you for being my ever merciful, loving Father. Thank you for your gift of love.

In Jesus' name,
Amen

Chapter 9
The Many Faces of Grief

Jesus Christ is the same yesterday and today and forever.
- Hebrews 13:8 (NIV)

You became sorrowful as God intended...Godly sorrow
brings repentance that leads to salvation and leaves no
regret, but worldly sorrow brings death.
- 2 Corinthians: 7:9-10 (NIV)

Cast all your anxiety on Him because he cares for you.
- 1 Peter 5:7 (NIV)

David had been gone for just a few months, but my grief started long before David's return to Heaven. In the bustle of details and daily life, I simply did not recognize it. To be honest, I was not even looking for it. I was just trying to survive. When I began looking at my grief head on, I realized that grief wears many faces and takes many forms. It does not follow a prescribed path or outlet. It is just a raw response to equally raw pain.

Grief also wears many labels of human words that attempt to name feelings so strong they overtake us: regret, fatigue, loss, lost, guilt, guilty, churning, sad, sorry, worry, worried, torture, agony, devastated, overwhelmed and (until recently) my theme song:

would've-should've-could've-didn't. Grief can be a cruel task master that pummels us into paralyzing hopelessness and agony that leaves us spent, shackled and disappointed by each new day. If we let it, it will overshadow God's hope and light. It gets in the way of our only hope. Then we feel lost and clamoring for God to come get us. Until I met Bootsie, that is precisely what I was doing.

My clamoring left me breathless and curled up emotionally. I wanted to lie down and stay down. Getting up only meant more beatings. I had given up. For the first time in my life, I was disappointed to wake up every day. Instead of praising the day the Lord had made, I started each day with the words, "I can't do this. I *don't want to* do this." I hated what I was letting happen to me. I hated me. I just wanted this world to stop. I even scoffed at my favorite Christian music and rolled my eyes at the testimonies of faith that were usually so comforting. I was done.

Blurs and New Beginnings

After David's return to Heaven, the rest of 2016 flew by in a blur and a flurry of events and more major life changes and skirmishes. The losses continued to mount. I continued to weaken and crumble. I simply ran *through* the fences now.

The day after David left, recent events dictated that I had to begin the process to renew the restraining order against his family member before the year expired. This chore interfered with my time and ability to focus on planning David's service. It was the last thing I needed to be dealing with at that time. Yet there it was.

The summer eroded quickly as I moved myself and our two remaining dogs to a new, smaller house outside of town. I raked myself with guilt over uprooting the dogs and making them live in a fishbowl neighborhood with few trees and not a single squirrel. I questioned every single decision and concluded that I was not being a good steward of the resources David provided for me – even though multiple financially sound people advised me otherwise. I just wanted to tear myself up and blame myself for something.

One of the most difficult tasks I faced was listing the house David and I had shared. For eight months, it remained unsold with only a handful of showings. It pained me to keep going back and forth to keep it presentable for showings. Seeing it empty, hearing the echoes and recalling memories always made me regret moving and the fresh start I thought I was attempting to make. I kept regretting leaving what we had there. I also continued to make mortgage payments on it and manage two homes. It was a shackle that held me back.

To complicate matters, I started a new school year with a new boss and a now hour-long commute. More changes and more stress manifested themselves in multiple physical issues that forced me to seek a job closer to home. As a result, I have lost my loving, supportive school family and the 600-little people who surrounded me with daily doses of love, smiles, and fun. More loss, more adjustment, more pain…

My rescuer waited.

Round One

The first time my grief assaulted me, the attack was bold and merciless – right there in broad daylight too. It was the kick-off ceremony to celebrate the new school year. I woke up tired, and I dreaded the large crowds and bustle those events always created. Those situations always drain my energy. Yet I went. It was required anyway, but I was trying to make it an important new beginning. I survived, but barely.

I had ridden to the event with some other teachers. One of the teachers asked if we could stop by the local livestock auction yard to pick up something for her father. As we waited for her to come back out, I looked up to see a young white calf being pushed into the fence rails by the squalling herd of other calves. I gasped for air and almost lost it. I could not speak the rest of the way to the parking lot where I had parked my car to meet the carpool. It was all I could do to not break down crying.

When we finally got back to the parking lot, I jumped out of the car without even speaking to the other teachers. My hands shook as I unlocked my car. Then I fell into the front seat into a heap of a gasping, sobbing human. All I could see when I closed my eyes was that young calf, fighting just to stand up. The abject cruelty of that poor calf's situation had opened the floodgates of my grief. I bawled and gasped for almost 30 minutes in my car. I headed straight home, fell onto the bed and cried my eyeballs out the rest of the afternoon. When I realized nobody even noticed that I had not returned to school after the ceremony, the tears cranked right up again. I can honestly say I have never cried that hard in my entire life.

I felt the life and hope drain out of me with my tears. I didn't care.

Similar situations frequently happened at school. Luckily the children did not see me crying. One particularly difficult day, I was overwhelmed by the volume of books I had to shelve between classes. My grief started as anger at having to give up my usual lunch time with the kids to shelve books. I felt unappreciated. I felt taken advantage of. I felt useless. Then I felt completely alone. I fell to the floor in the corner where I was shelving books and just started bawling and gasping for air. I had always read about "hot tears" coursing down a character's face. I now knew what that meant. My tears were not restricted to one or two at a time. My tears fell in liquid sheets. I didn't know one human could produce that much water at one time. I raced for my office and tried to pull myself together before my next class. I just wanted to go home - for good.

Total Knock Out (TKO)

If you look up the words "foster failures" you probably will see a picture of David and me. Through various dog rescue efforts over the years, David and I had gotten to know several Great Dane rescue volunteers. They knew we had lost Kittie to cancer earlier that year. They also knew we loved Great Danes and would rescue anything. We were softies and could not refuse the chance to help a dog in need – and they knew it. They sent an e-mail to ask if we could take in a Dane because they were out of foster homes. Attached was a picture of a tall skinny dog with gray and black swirls – blue merle, they call it. It was Wednesday. He was scheduled to be euthanized on Friday. I instantly said, "YES!" Then I told David who, of course, agreed.

When Tillman came to us, he had no name. He had been picked up wandering the streets of Greenville, SC. A few days after we agreed to keep him, Tillman arrived. He was strapped in the bucket seat of a little pick-up truck. It makes me smile now to think of my first glimpse of him in the back seat. Out clambered a friendly, albeit extremely thin, dog. It hurt my feelings for him when his rescuer said, "You don't have to keep him if you don't want him."

I thought, *He is wonderful. How could anyone not want him? How could we even think of giving him up?*

We brought him in the house and let him explore. Then we put him in a giant cage that took up the whole middle of the kitchen. Luckily we only needed the cage until Tillman was house-trained. After a few days of stomach issues and figuring out his place in the pack, Tillman had settled in.

We named Tillman after one of the founders of Clemson University because David and his dad both went there. I told David we needed a Clemson connection. So "Tillman" it was. David called him "T-Man" for short. I called Tillman "The Big Silly" and "Bubba Silly" ("Bubba" for short) because he was the quintessential male Great Dane – goofy, klutzy, mischievous and a true comedian. I thanked him for making our hearts bigger every day.

Tillman's antics brought us such joy every single day. He loved pillows and quickly took over the head of the bed – sideways, of course, which left David and me clinging to the two inches of bed that was left. He was a counter surfer. He thought couch pillows were a delicacy.

He was a voracious reader who shredded a bunch of my books. He snitched garden gloves if they weren't on my hands. He would snatch a plastic bag, masks, sticks or anything he could grab. Then he'd just bolt around the yard, inviting anyone to chase him.

Twice, I had made the mistake of planting a blueberry bush in what ended up being part of his runway when the zoomies would overtake him and compel him to circle the yard in a cloud of dust. He would zip by me – narrowly missing me – with the biggest grin on his face and tongue just lolling. One time he clipped me at the ankles and sent me straight up in the air and over like a tree. I was unhurt – probably because I was laughing so hard. Ah, Tillman…Needless to say, by the time he returned to Heaven, my Bubba Silly was nothing like that little bag of bones and hesitant puppy that entered our life. *Thank you, God.*

Tillman

When the Lights Went Out

After Tillman returned to Heaven, I turned on myself with a vengeance. Once again, I accused myself of messing everything up and making others suffer because of my ineptitude. We should've had his leg amputated sooner. I did not give Tillman enough attention and love.

He hurt because of me. He suffered because of me. I told myself the same things about David. I spent too much time away from home. I didn't shield him enough from my overwhelming stress. I never should have taken that job. I didn't make them feel loved...My boxing soundtrack continued in an endless loop. When was it going to stop?

I even blamed myself for Tillman and David not coming back to "visit" me in my dreams like Kittie and the others did. I told myself: *Who can blame them? I wouldn't want to come back here either...I don't deserve them.* I was so desperately overwhelmed and thirsting for peace, I was turning to my dreams to ease my suffering. Meanwhile, God waited.

Night time was the worst. Sometimes I even fought to avoid sleeping. I had been having stress dreams for quite a while already. I never could recall details of most of them, but I would wake up crying so I knew whatever I dreamt was not a happy event. So far, David has only come to visit me in two dreams.

When David first stepped into my dreams, he was with me at the new house. I could not see him. I just knew it was him. I was suddenly grasping and holding onto his legs simply bawling and crying. Though I said nothing, I felt like I was wailing and begging inside: *Please don't leave me!* Then I woke up. I opened my eyes to a gush of tears.

In the second dream, the emaciated, weak David appeared. He and I were talking to some first responders (firemen, I think). David was explaining in his weak, wispy emaciated voice, "We've just had so much suffering lately." Then he fell down in a crumpled heap. I knelt beside him, and his eyes moved slowly up to look into mine. He raised his head by holding his chin between his right thumb and forefinger - a habit he had developed shortly after treatment because of his extremely weakened muscles. Those ghostly eyes held my gaze. He said in his weak, old man voice, "I guess I need to put on my noisy overcoat." All I could do was stroke his head and cry, saying over and over, "I know. I know." Once again, I woke up to tears pouring down my face.

For months and months I waited for Tillman.

A Hope and a Future

I often think about little Bootsie – the stray who brought me back to God and re-lit my life's pilot light. His fear kept him away from the very ones who would give him what he so desperately sought: food, water, warmth - and rest. His fear kept him torn between the dark, cold woods and the comfort of a clean house and the gentle hand of a rescuer. I can honestly say I have been there. I truly understand how Bootsie felt.

Only when I gave myself permission to get in there and box with my grief – to feel every stinging bite of it – could I understand and diffuse it. Only when I can turn my grief and sorrow over to God and truly let it go may I may find peace and closure. It was finally okay to be angry. Being angry used to mean I was weak and unhappy. Now it was an acceptable response. Even Jesus got angry. I remember David saying that quite often – that "even Jesus got angry. Look what he did to the tax agents." Even Jesus asked God to take his suffering from him.

It was okay to rail at God and tell him I found the plan confounding and downright unacceptable. It finally hit me, and I started telling myself that it was okay - that God understood our human emotions. What I needed to realize was when to let them go and not let them keep me from Him anymore. They certainly didn't help matters. So why not let them go and give them to God? He could take it. Through my seemingly endless trials, I have realized that, even amid the changing faces of grief, Jesus Christ never changes. He is still right there, waiting patiently, loving me through every blow and tear.

Heavenly Father and Christ Jesus, my Lord, I pray:

Thank you for being a God of second chances. Thank you for having a sense of humor and loving us enough to make sure we smile every day. Thank you for Tillman and the countless others who bring smiles and make our hearts bigger every day. Thank you for helping me to recognize and know love and especially how it feels when it fills my heart to overflowing. I look forward to the day when those I have loved meet me at the door one last time and forever more. There is no greater gift than to reach that day when we all will live in the light of your grace and love – together again forever more.

In Jesus' name,
Amen

Chapter 10
Living in the Echo

Yet it was good of you to share in my troubles...My God will meet all your needs according to his glorious riches in Christ Jesus.
- Philippians 4:15, 19 (NIV)

And at the ninth hour Jesus cried out in a loud voice, "My God, my God, why have you forsaken me?"
Mark 15:34 (NIV)

I know what it is to be in need, and I know what it is to have plenty. I have learned the secret of being content in any and every situation, whether well fed or hungry, whether living in plenty or in want. I can do everything through him who gives me strength.
- Philippians 4:12-13 (NIV)

David would often assert that everything would be fine. He truly believed God would make all things right and provide for our every need. I think that is why he had so few needs and rarely wanted anything more than he had. He always seemed content. Was he perfect? Did he bear his adversity without complaint? No. He hurt – a lot. Did he question the plan? Of course he did. Did he wonder why God had forsaken him? Yes. Even that. Yet what made David unique was that those moments were few and far between – at least as far as anyone could see – and even in the midst of adversity he rested in the knowledge that God was in control. Even at the peak of David's physical suffering, he believed a larger plan was at work. Even when he knew his time was growing small, he reached out to others. He so wanted to bring others to Christ. He sought always to do God's will and live as Jesus did.

David's return to Heaven remains the most significant loss in my life. I miss him daily. About seven months after David's departure, I happened to hear Michael Bublé's version of the song, *This Love of Mine*.[xxiv] All I could do was cry. It is a beautiful song, and very beautifully choreographed – the perfect movie music – but I felt like it was talking about me: David is "always on my mind though out of sight." I feel a void that nobody and nothing can fill. Even though I am surrounded family, church friends, my dogs, and my students and friends, my days feel lonesome. The nights are even worse. I "cried my heart out." I have felt it break. "Nothing mattered." So, I "let it break." The love I have for David had nowhere to go. What was I supposed to do with all this love of mine? That is exactly where I was.

I was becoming an automaton just going through the motions of living, but I wasn't living. The way I saw it, I was not even existing. I did not want to.

Paying It Forward

David was a generous man who always gave to others even when his own resources were limited. I recall a story he sometimes told me about going to a co-worker's Christmas party. Everyone was supposed to bring an ornament. David's contribution was simple and inexpensive, but he had put some thought into it. When he arrived at the party, he saw a huge glistening Christmas tree in the foyer - full of expensive ornaments. He placed his simple offering on the tree, but he immediately felt out of place. So he left. Sweet David! Sometimes I would wonder about that little ornament. I picture David's thoughtful gift being swallowed up and lost among the voluminous plenty of expensive, shiny ornaments. Did the party's host and hostess appreciate it? Did they even notice it? Do they still have it? Whatever became of it?

That story used to make me hurt for David. It overwhelmed my heart with love for him. So I would always hug him when he told it. What a gentle-hearted man he was! David continued to pay it forward, always stepping in to help others. I have a tender heart, too, and I often give and sacrifice for others, but from David I learned how to be quietly bold with my gifts. I am better for having known and loved David – and for being known and loved by David. *Thank you, God.*

Now What?

After seven months of drag-down grief and exhaustion and mentally giving up, I tried to re-focus my energies off of myself and onto others. After all, that had always worked in the past whenever I was feeling mired down by my own circumstances. Focusing on other people's adversity and traumas used to put my own circumstances into a better perspective. So I gave. I gave to church. I gave to multiple charities. I bought books and bean bag chairs for my students. I bought coats and clothes for needy children. I bought a meal for the car behind me in the drive-through line. I paid compliments to others. I checked on friends in need. I prayed for others. Reaching outside of myself had always pulled me out of the quick-sand. Not this time. Nothing was working. Not even that. Then along came Bootsie.

Bootsie re-focused me. Bootsie helped me answer the nagging question: *So, what happens to one's love when the object of that affection is no longer present? Where does it go?* It definitely needs an outlet, and I had given it many. Then I realized as I scoured my neighborhood for Bootsie that giving love to others is only part of the answer. What about an inlet? I understood then what my Hospice counselor had been saying - that I needed to love myself too. I was so touched by that ironically humble realization I stopped the car and bowed my head in prayer. Suddenly it was okay to love myself too. I needed to share some of my love with myself for a change. I finally gave myself permission. I could not move forward until I did that.

I always had been afraid that loving myself meant that I would become arrogant, selfish and self-centered. I have tried so hard, so deliberately, to be the complete opposite of those terms, I think I went so far in the other direction that I had lost sight of myself – and especially God. All I felt was unworthy. I could do nothing right. I never knew where the lines were.

I am still an amateur at giving myself permission to love myself, but doing so keeps me aware of God's gentle hand on me. It felt so good. No longer was I berating myself for everything and blaming myself for undesirable outcomes. I was learning. I started re-programming myself. And the Lord said, "That's good." *Thank you, God.*

The Echo

The events of the last few months have prompted me to wonder: What happens to a person's love after he passes on? Where does that person's love go? Do they take it with them? These questions have stumbled around in my heart for a while now. I still puzzle about them, but it is becoming clear. Any love we share in this world is never in vain. It remains behind. David's love is still here in this world. His love appears in every person he touched – even strangers he passed who never even knew his name. David's drops of love have rippled out wider than he ever knew. It comforts me to think he knows that now.

I am still alone in this world. I still make all the big decisions and plan for my survival. Happily, now being alone does not feel as raw as it had gotten during my darkest days. My days can still be lonesome, but I still am surrounded by love – from David and from my dearest four-legged angels and loved ones who have transitioned to the place we all hope to be someday. I know with a calm certainty and peace that I am never really alone – just as Bootsie was never really alone out there in the dark woods. Instead of breaking further, my heart is starting to heal. *Thank you, God.*

Heavenly Father and Christ Jesus, my Lord, I pray...

Thank you for your love and companionship. Thank you for the echo for it turns me to you. Only when I have emptied out the distractions and trappings of grief can I truly focus on you and what you ask of us. Thank you for filling the echo with certainty, blessed peace and the assurance that the silences and sufferings in this world are not forever. They are but part of your plan for me. Thank you for delivering hope and a future with you. May your promise fill me with joy and a quiet obedience to your will and plan.

In Jesus' name,
Amen

Chapter 11
The Gift List

We are hard pressed on every side, but not crushed;
perplexed, but not in despair; persecuted, but not
abandoned; struck down, but not destroyed...life is at
work in you...So we fix our eyes not on what is seen, but
on what is unseen. For what is seen is temporary, but
what is unseen is eternal.
- 2 Corinthians: 4:8-9, 12, 18 (NIV)

"My grace is sufficient for you, for my power is made
perfect in weakness."
- 2 Corinthians 12: 9 (NIV)

And we know that in all things God works for the good of
those who love him, who have been called according to
His purpose...If God is for us, who can be against us?...
In all these things we are more than conquerors through
Him who loved us. For I am convinced that neither death
nor life, neither angels nor demons, neither the present
nor the future, nor any powers, neither height nor depth,
nor anything else in all creation, will be able to separate
us from the love of God that is in Christ Jesus our Lord.
- Romans 8:28, 10, 37-39 (NIV)

David was a gift - a bright light in this world. He
still is. His love still is. All he wanted was for Jesus to

recognize his efforts and sacrifices. When I recall the sudden smile on David's face as he left us, I think he finally – after years of sacrifice, adversity and months of physical suffering – looked upon the face he sought for so long. What a comforting image! David with his Lord Jesus Christ – free of pain and warmed by God's love. The ultimate gift!

God appeared many times along David's journey. He appeared many times during my journey and the years after it. God worked through so many people. They held us up, they comforted us, they fed us, they cried with us. We appreciated every one of them and their gifts along the way. However, it is in looking back at the journey that I see how every single one of them was a lifeline to God. They radiated His grace and unquenchable love for us, reminding us that all was not lost – that a greater plan was at work – and that all was for our good.

Comforts and Blessings

Countless kindnesses shown to David and me throughout our life's journey have seen me to this point. Finally, in spite of adversity and pain of the last several years, I can claim a heart of gratitude. Instead of the "Hit List" I now have a "Gift List." The gifts we received are timeless and provide comfort in all situations. We received them with open and grateful hearts.

People are essentially good. Situations like David's journey bring out the best in them. They want to help. I needed to let them. I was so glad I did because it opened up possibilities and friendships and countless quiet moments of hope and love. Many people offered suggestions about other treatment options: enzymes, trials, herbs, music, immunotherapy and others. They did not mean to question our doctors. They were just trying to help. We let them.

Shortly after his diagnosis, one of David's mother's cousins sent what will remain the most special gift of all – a simple wooden cross and a prayer shawl. Both of these simple gifts provided more comfort to David throughout his journey than a whole pharmacy of pain medications could. He held the cross in his hand as he smilingly transitioned to greet his Lord and Savior, Jesus Christ. It was the first item I moved into my new home. It still stands on my counter and greets me every day.

Our wonderful church family stepped up immediately with meals, prayers, and help around the house. They drove David to doctor's appointments so I could go to work. There are not enough pages to list everything they did to hold us up. On one particularly cold day when the forecast predicted the possibility of ice, someone had asked, "What about the Fricks?" That simple question opened the floodgates, and suddenly we had a generator on our back porch. We also were included as one of the families to get assistance during our church's annual "Fixing It for Christ" program. I had mentioned to someone that I could not handle cleaning our home's exterior. So, in 100-degree heat, our loving church friends cleaned posts and repaired and repainted porch rails. The next year, they answered yet again – cleaning the outside and repairing interior drywall and trim-work, and replacing the front door light fixture so I could put the house on the market. I love my church family!

Throughout David's battle, insurance and medical costs were a constant thorn in our side. My brother-in-law, Jim, established a GoFundMe page for us. Our loving church family sponsored a BBQ benefit dinner to raise funds to ease that burden. Between just those two efforts, Jim and our church family raised enough funds to help us make the transition until my new employer's health insurance took effect. I will never forget walking into the fellowship hall and seeing the crowd that had gathered. As soon as friends caught sight of me and David, they rose in a mob and rushed over to hug and love us. David was so overwhelmed he began to cry and had to step into the men's room to collect himself. He could not believe all of that was done for him. He felt so loved. *Thank you, God.*

At David's service, our church family one again answered by surrounding me and David's family with an outpouring of love I will never forget. The church was packed. Jim delivered a touching eulogy. Pastor John delivered a message of David's journey, his heart of service - and especially his strong faith and love for Jesus. My nephews, sisters and family were with me. I felt completely surrounded by love and caring hearts. Sometimes when doubt flickers in, all I have to do is remember that day and all the love that was present there in one place at one time. Then I no longer feel lost. I know without question that David was loved – as am I.

The staff at Ballantyne Veterinary Hospital also recognized our need and went above and beyond to help us help our Tillman through his journey and last days. They filled every prescription for Tillman's pain meds – sometimes at the last minute. They always made time for us. I lost count of how many times Dr. Humphrey adjusted his schedule so he could drive to the house and help me load Tillman into the car. He even followed me back home to help me unload Tillman. He coordinated with a local vet to use their x-ray facilities so Tillman did not have to travel as far. He called the cremation service to coordinate Tillman's pick up and cremation. Dr. Humphrey was there at the end to comfort us. I was so touched when he thanked *us* for allowing him to be part of our journey.

God's Time, Not Mine

Finally, the Waxhaw house sold. The closing date was Tuesday, March 21, 2017 – exactly one year after David's return to Heaven. My realtor said most real estate closings happen on a Thursday or Friday. She also told me that in all the years she has been in real estate, only a handful of her closings ever occurred on a Tuesday. Apparently, our buyers specifically requested March 21 - a Tuesday. At the closing, my part took all of 15 minutes, and the closing attorney happened to be a Clemson graduate. Coincidence? I think not! I took the closing date and other happy events as one clear sign from David (and God) that I was on the right path after all. What was happening was what God wanted to happen. It was His plan, His time – not mine. Once again, He showed me I could trust Him implicitly to take care of everything. I could let go. *Thank you, God.*

Unlikely Heroes

As always, our fur angels administered to our needs and provided constant comfort at every turn. Lucy and Pup continued to make our hearts bigger despite our attempts to let the constrictions take over our hearts whenever the road got long, treacherous and dark. During David's last couple days, sweet soft Lucy remained by David's side, only leaving him to eat or go outside. She had done the same thing with Kittie. She just knew. *Thank you, God.*

Nurse Lucy on Duty

Pup

Lucy

The sweet little bird nest in our front door light fixture where the glass insert had been made everyone smile as they entered and left our home. Everyone enjoyed watching the birds figure out the best way to build their nest. David's mom and dad and I tried to help them by creating a platform to catch the pieces of twigs, grass and dog hair that kept falling down. It took a nurse, an engineer and a school librarian to figure out how to affix a shallow plastic container to the light fixture. Turns out the birds didn't need our help anyway. They had piled up all manner of nesting materials on the floor under the light. We all chuckled at the little construction zone that had cropped up on the front porch. What a lovely distraction those little birds were! It was a joy to see new life blooming even at the end of another.

Along the way, David and I talked about me getting a horse and taking riding lessons again. David wanted me to have something that got me out of the house once in a while. My wee prince, Blaze, has certainly done that! My little hunny pot makes me smile every day. At the barn where I boarded Blaze at that time, I met Kim and her horse, Maximus – a gigantic, 18-year-old Tennessee Walker. The day after David's departure, I escaped to the barn for some aromatherapy and a quiet cry with Blaze. When I got there, big ol' Maximus whickered at me from his stall at the end of the aisle and stuck his head over his half-door. He had never done that before. I could not resist his gentle invitation to let him comfort me too. He knew what I needed and when.

Blaze

Special Visitors

As always, God works in many wonderful ways. One particularly fun dream and yet another dog helped me find a sense of closure about David and Tillman. Both events reminded me that God is still at work even if I am standing still (on the rare occasion that I actually do stand still) – and especially despite my unintentional, human efforts to interfere with His plans.

Although David was reserved most of the time, he had the most infectious laugh when he got going. I wish I had a recording of it because it makes me smile now just thinking about it. When David belly-laughed, he would start with a shake and then just go to town – doubling over and laughing to the point of losing his breath or wiping tears of laughter from his eyes – almost wailing with laughter. It was hysterical. He invariably would try to talk while laughing which only made him shake and laugh harder. We were blessed with many moments when he laughed like that. I was blessed recently to hear it again – albeit only in my dreams.

David chose a few days before Clemson cinched the 2016 College Football National Championship to visit me in a dream. He was the full-sized, healthy David, and he was doubled over - laughing hysterically at something. We both were. I like to think it was because he knew his beloved Tigers would finally take the championship and get the respect he always believed they deserved. Even though it was a short part of an all- too-short dream, that laugh was a beautiful thing to hear again. It makes me smile now just thinking about it. I don't know what we were laughing at. I suppose it doesn't really matter. We were together. We were laughing. That's one dream I wish I could replay.

Tillman finally came back to visit me, too, but he showed up in person (or in-dog) through a little dog I will call Tilly – a Catahoula Hound Dog. It was a few days before my first Christmas without David and Tillman. When I met Tilly, she was running into traffic on a busy highway. Another driver and I pulled over to help get her out of the road. Tilly was so scared, she belly-crawled over to me - with a little grin on her face. At first I was unsure if she was snarling at me, but then I saw how submissive the rest of her was. Sure enough, when she got to me, she simply flopped over on her back – just in time for a semi tractor trailer to crawl by us. Then I got my first good look at her. I had seen those swirls before. I had seen that face. I was looking at a much smaller version of my beloved Tillman. I almost cried right there in the highway when that occurred to me.

The other rescuer was unable to take Tilly with her so we opened my car door, and Tilly hopped right in and made herself at home. She looked up at me and stayed close – always touching me. I talked to her and petted her – and fell in love. I took her to a local vet for a flea treatment and rabies shot. Then I took her home, thanking God for crossing my paths with such a sweet creation.

Tilly made herself at home on my bed (much to Pup's dismay) – and everywhere else, including my heart. The more time she spent with me, the more I realized that she was a special Christmas visitor. Not only did Tilly look like my Tillman, she sounded like him. She whined like him. She acted like him. She had the same soft ears and wild swirls. She even smelled like him. I had to fight back tears when I first buried my face in her warm, soft ears and realized I knew that smell – the same soft, warm butter smell as Tillman's.

Shortly after I found Tilly, a fellow rescuer had posted news of my little treasure on a local website to see if anyone was looking for a lost dog. I knew someone had to be missing her. She was clean and obviously used to being in the house. While I knew that was true, I also hoped nobody would claim her. But…someone did. Tilly's person contacted me the next day. So I just enjoyed the day with her and hoped her person would be late picking her up. He is a very nice man who explained how Tilly (a.k.a., "Bonnie") had escaped her invisible fencing. Her brother, Clyde, had pulled off her collar when they were playing. He asked if I had seen her "grin" yet. He described what a bed-hog she is (which I had already discovered the hard way). He even offered to let me come visit her, but we have not been able to connect for a play time yet.

On one hand, I felt like I had lost Tillman again, but on the other, I knew I had been blessed with a very special Christmas visitor who brought me some much needed Christmas comfort and joy. She knew I was missing somebody. Even though I still miss her, I am happy knowing that she is back at home where she belongs. Little Tilly/Bonnie was only with me for one night, but she is in my heart forever – right next to Tillman. I still miss my Tillman, of course, but (thanks to little Bonnie) that void doesn't feel as deep or sharp.

Then, finally, after many months, Tillman also visited me in my dreams for some warm snuggle time – just like we had enjoyed countless times before. Another dream I wish I could replay!

"Tilly"   *Tillman*

One Last Hug

David used to joke that he never knew when Easter was. Sometimes at Christmas he would joke about it being Easter. Ironically (or not), David returned to Heaven right before Easter. What perfect timing. God's perfect timing. What a comfort it is to remember that. How much more special Easter has become!

David and I had many special moments during and after his treatment. One moment that makes me smile happened shortly after we had called Hospice in to help me with David's increased needs and his care. The

Hospice nurse and I were helping David get back in bed. We were trying to adjust his pajama bottoms, but we were struggling because David could not stand up without help anymore. The nurse told David to lean on me. I told David to just hang onto me. He leaned into me, and his long arms encircled me in a long, sweet hug. He whispered in his now weak, wispy voice, "I love you." I heard the nurse exclaim, "Aw! You guys are so sweet." I told David I loved him too and just held on. I am so glad I held on and paused time even for a few extra seconds because it did not occur to me just then that it would be our last hug.

Heavenly Father and Christ Jesus, my Lord, I pray...

Thank you for many special moments with David. Thank you for the realization of how special they were and always will be. Thank you for the countless gifts and friendships that appear exactly when I need them. Thank you for the love that lives with me here and especially for the love I will leave behind when you call me home. Please help me be better with each day. May I show your love to this fallen world in my every action and deed. May I recognize opportunities to hold others closely and show them your comfort during times of trial and adversity. I invite you with a grateful heart and love into my heart and life. I cannot survive without your grace and the promise that only you offer and sustain for my good and my future.

In Jesus' name, Amen

Chapter 12
Finishing the Race

*There is a time for everything, and a season for every
activity under heaven.*
- Ecclesiastes 3:1 (NIV)

Though He slay me, I will hope in Him.
- Job 13:15 (NIV)

*Trust in the Lord with all your heart and lean not on your
own understanding;*
*In all your ways acknowledge him, and he will make your
paths straight.*
- Proverbs 3:5-6 (NIV)

Those who hope in the Lord will renew their strength.
They will soar on wings like
*Eagles; they will run and not grow weary, they will walk
and not be faint.*
- Isaiah 40:31 (NIV)

David understood that love is a progression. First
we must have faith in a generous and loving God and that
Jesus Christ died so that we would be saved and able to
bask in the love God and Jesus for all eternity. We must
trust in the Lord with all of our heart. We must turn all
things over to Him who loves us. Then we find and grow
our hope – in God's plan – in the good as well as the

adversities and pain. Then comes love – truly the greatest of these. When we love in all things, we honor the Lord in all things. Isn't that what God asks of us? It is beautifully simple, but we stray humans complicate the formula by asking questions and taking our eyes off of Jesus. Sometimes it is only in the adversity and twists and turns of this life's journey that we emerge with greater love and acceptance of God's plan for us.

Our heavenly Father assures us that "There is a time for everything, and a season for every activity under heaven" (Ecclesiastes 3:1). Clearly, I have been toiling through an especially long season of hardship. Just looking at my *Hit List* makes me tired. All of those things that have a season have presented themselves and challenged me – sometimes mercilessly. I have wanted to lie down and quit getting up. The dark and cold fingers of hopelessness have clutched at my heart. I have felt my hope and faith dimming.

After David's death and the impending fallout, my ability to pick up the pieces to find happiness and the upside of even the darkest situations began to erode. When I'd hear the sweet bluegrass strands of Ralph Stanley's *I'll Fly Away,* I would interject with deep and earnest sarcasm, "Not soon enough…" Instead of rejoicing at each new day that the Lord had made, I was bitterly disappointed to wake up every day because every day held more of the same suffering and hardship.[xxv]

However, God instructs us to find happiness in spite of the toil:

> *"There is nothing better for men than to be happy and do good while they live. That everyone may eat and drink, and find satisfaction in all his toil –*

this is the gift of God...So I saw that there is
nothing better for a man than to enjoy his work,
because that is his lot. "
- Ecclesiastes 3: 12-13, 22 *(NIV)*

We are instructed to "cast all your anxiety on Him
because he cares for you" (1 Peter 5:7). I have recited that
Scripture often in times of need and adversity. I realize
now that I had overlooked one little word – "all." We are
supposed to cast *all* of our anxiety on Him, not just pieces
of it. We must turn it *all* over to Him. He promises He
will lift us up in due time. We just have to wait patiently,
seeking Him always.

I never truly understood that until Bootsie ran into
my life. Until I envisioned God as a rescuer, sitting
patiently, waiting for me to come to him willingly and
quietly, I simply could not do it anymore. I could not
handle all the grief I was carrying. If this much suffering
was a gift, I wanted no more heavenly gifts. All I could do
was scoff at the thought. My human self demanded a
return policy. Until I started seeing the seemingly endless,
egregiously unfair amount of toil, trauma and trials as
gifts, I was overwhelmed - indeed paralyzed - by fatigue,
anger and hopelessness. Now I am coming up for air. In
fact, as I type, my phone's playlist insists on re-playing
Louis Armstrong's rendition of *Whistle While You Work*
multiple times.[xxvi] I love it when God winks at me.

So I Wait...

When I look back at David's journey, I realize
how much we waited – waiting for a prognosis, in waiting

rooms, in hospital emergency rooms, waiting for scan results, waiting for the day we would hear that there was nothing else to be done. Finally, we waited expectantly for Jesus. When I thought about waiting on the Lord, I wondered what it really meant. When I envisioned God as a rescuer who waits for me, I wondered how the waiting worked. If I was waiting for Him, and He was waiting for me, how did we close the gap? Who was supposed to blink first? How long is the stalemate supposed to last? How do we bridge the ground between?

Then ironically (or not), I read *How to Let God Solve Your Problems* by Dr. Charles F. Stanley. Dr. Stanley defines *waiting* differently. He asserts:

> "Most people's idea of waiting is to just sit around doing nothing, but this is *not* what the Bible means when it speaks of waiting upon the Lord. From God's perspective, *waiting* is an action verb. This means it is alive with faith. During difficult times, we must trust God to bring us through the problem, trial, or tragedy. We may think that we are not gaining ground, but we are. In fact, from his viewpoint, we are gaining the most important ground because we are learning to trust Him in the darkest moments of our lives." (35-36)[xxvii]

> "Waiting for His best means you are willing to remain right where you are until you sense Him leading you on to the next step. It is an act of obedience, which always leads to blessing. This is why it involves faith." (36)[xxviii]

Dr. Stanley's definition comforts me because it helps me now see that waiting is an active but gentle process which keeps us close to God. We must truly be still and trust. That is when we come to life – literally – to the life that only our heavenly Father can offer.

Will That Be Takeout or Delivery?

When David and I waited for Jesus, I had company. I still had David. I am still waiting for Jesus. Now I may walk much of my journey by myself (physically-speaking), but I have the peace that our moments of waiting instilled in me. I also have the assurance that God and my Lord Jesus Christ and the blessed Holy Spirit walk with me. I am not alone. I need to say that again. *I am not alone.* While I wait, I look forward to where God will lead my steps. I know that God will meet me wherever I am. I simply need to rest until He lights my next steps.

Waiting is an active process of give and take – and ultimately of trust. Sometimes we wait at the counter for our order. Sometimes God delivers it without us even asking. Just as David finally got his ultimate wish when he called out to Jesus, I know God and Jesus and the Holy Spirit will answer. The best part is the knowledge that they love me through every moment of loss, suffering, and grief. They also will celebrate my victories. They will smile when I smile. They will rest with me in the quiet times. They will love what I love…even the black olives.

Thank you, God.

Heavenly Father and Christ Jesus, my Lord, I pray...

Thank you for being my rock, my salvation, my great deliverer and defender. Thank you for showing me the way back to you. Thank you for not letting me truly fall. Thank you for carrying me when I am too weak to stand. May I always know the comfort of your loving presence and promise.

In Jesus' name,
Amen

Bibliography

Armstrong, Louis. (1996). "Whistle While You Work." On *Disney Songs the Satchmo Way* [CD]. Burbank, CA: Buena Vista Pictures Distribution.

Boyle, Susan Boyle. (2010). "Make Me a Channel of Your Peace." On *The Gift* [CD]. London, England: Simco Ltd. Under exclusive license to Sony BMG Music Entertainment.

Bublé, Michael. (2016). "This Love of Mine." On *Nobody But Me (Deluxe Version)* [CD]. Burbank, CA: Reprise Records, a division of Warner Brothers Records.

Mitchell, Margaret. (1973). *Gone with the Wind.* New York: Avon Books (p. 708).

Scofield, C.I. (ed.). (1984). Oxford NIV Scofield Study Bible. New York: Oxford University Press.

Stanley, C.F. (2008). *How to Let God Solve Your Problems.* Nashville, TN: Thomas Nelson (pp. 35-36).

Stanley, Ralph. (2005). "I'll Fly Away." On *Shine On.* [CD]. Charlottesville, VA: Rebel Records, LLC.

Endnotes

[i] Mitchell, Margaret. (1973). *Gone with the Wind.* New York: Avon Books (p. 708).

[ii] Boyle, Susan Boyle. (2010). "Make Me a Channel of Your Peace." On *The Gift* [CD]. London, England: Simco Ltd. Under exclusive license to Sony BMG Music Entertainment.

[iii] Frick, Marie. "Re: A Favor for David." Message to P.J. Frick. January 27, 2016. E-mail.

[iv] Fenske, Johnny. "Re: A Favor for David." Message to P.J. Frick. January 2016. E-mail.

[v] Johnson, Susan. "Re: A Favor for David." Message to P.J. Frick. January 2016. E-mail.

[vi] Spencer, Scott. "Re: A Favor for David." Message to P.J. Frick. January 2016. E-mail.

[vii] Traver, Susan and Al. "Re: A Favor for David." Message to P.J. Frick. January 2016. E-mail.

[viii] Morgan, Becky. "Re: A Favor for David." Message to P.J. Frick. January 2016. E-mail.

[ix] Anzaldi, Lee. "Re: A Favor for David." Message to P.J. Frick. January 2016. E-mail.

[x] McGill, John. "Re: A Favor for David." Message to P.J. Frick. January 2016. E-mail.

xi Gordon, Janet. "Re: A Favor for David." Message to P.J. Frick. January 2016. E-mail.

xii Dussinger, Pat. "Re: A Favor for David." Message to P.J. Frick. January 2016. E-mail.

xiii Morton, Kim. "Re: A Favor for David." Message to P.J. Frick. January 2016. E-mail.

xiv Hiate, Bonnie. "Re: A Favor for David." Message to P.J. Frick. January 2016. E-mail.

xv Lockamy, Kathy. "Re: A Favor for David." Message to P.J. Frick. January 2016. E-mail.

xvi Huelsman, Ann. "Re: A Favor for David." Message to P.J. Frick. January 2016. E-mail.

xvii Davidson, Carmen. "Re: A Favor for David." Message to P.J. Frick. January 2016. E-mail.

xviii Moorman, Nick. "Re: A Favor for David." Message to P.J. Frick. January 2016. E-mail.

xix Moorman, Ron. "Re: A Favor for David." Message to P.J. Frick. January 2016. E-mail.

xx McClellan, Phyllis. "Re: A Favor for David." Message to P.J. Frick. January 2016. E-mail.

xxi Lord, Janet. "Re: A Favor for David." Message to P.J. Frick. February 12, 2016. E-mail.

[xxii] Mcgill, Anita. "Re: A Note to David." Message to P.J. Frick. December 18, 2015. E-mail.

[xxiii] Denny, Jim. "Re: A Favor for David." Message to P.J. Frick. January 2016. E-mail.

[xxiv] Bublé, Michael. (2016). "This Love of Mine." On *Nobody But Me (Deluxe Version)* [CD]. Burbank, CA: Reprise Records, a division of Warner Brothers Records.

[xxv] Stanley, Ralph. (2005). "I'll Fly Away." On *Shine On.* [CD]. Charlottesville, VA: Rebel Records, LLC.

[xxvi] Armstrong, Louis. (1996). "Whistle While You Work." On *Disney Songs the Satchmo Way* [CD]. Burbank, CA: Buena Vista Pictures Distribution.

[xxvii] Stanley, C.F. (2008). *How to Let God Solve Your Problems.* Nashville, TN: Thomas Nelson, p. 35.

[xxviii] Stanley, C.F., p. 36.

CPSIA information can be obtained
at www.ICGtesting.com
Printed in the USA
FSOW03n1700081017
39618FS

9 780692 941201